Life Trails

Finding God's Presence In Our World

A Collection of Devotions By Dave Kranz

DAVE KRANZ CREATIONS

Thank You

This collection of devotions is dedicated to God who has patiently helped me grow closer to Him over time. These writings truly are gifts from Him. They pretty much wrote themselves in spurts over the last 15 years. He placed numerous people in my path, and provided a wonderful church home, resulting in a faith that has brought much joy to my life.

Many people have contributed to this family project. No one deserves more credit than Carolyn Kranz, my angel of a wife. As an earthly angel she was my encourager and editor. She took rough sentences and choppy thought processes then edited them to sensibility. As a heavenly angel she has become my inspiration and faith hero. This book would not have been published without the help of my good friend Kim Waltman. An incredible wordsmith, his editing augmented my limited vocabulary and corrected my imperfect structure. Patricia Kranz and Tracey Weaver also contributed their editing skills. Without the help and encouragement of these people, these devotions would be buried away in my computer, inspiring no one.

Many of the messages and ideas were inspired by sermons given at Hosanna! Church in Lakeville Minnesota. Chapters three and four are the result of writings for our yearly men's retreats. My small group members were wonderful encouragers who helped hone my gifts by providing a safe place to grow in my spirituality. But none deserves more credit than God. I thank you Lord for giving me the gift of hearing your voice. May this book help others hear it also.

Philippians 4:4–7
"Always be full of joy in the Lord. I say it again—rejoice! Let everyone see that you are considerate in all you do. Remember, the Lord is coming soon. Don't worry about anything; instead, pray about everything. Tell God what you need, and thank him for all he has done. Then you will experience God's peace, which exceeds anything we can understand. His peace will guard your hearts and minds as you live in Christ Jesus."

What People are Saying About <u>Life Trails.</u>

Bill Bohline—Founding pastor of Hosanna! Church.

"Dave Kranz is my friend and he will be your friend, too, as soon as you start to read. He has a keen eye, a creative mind, a knowledge of science, and a love for the Lord. All these combine to give you insight and inspiration, page after page. Enjoy the journey—Dave has the ability to take you places even as you relax in a comfortable chair and receive each blessing."

Pat Moe—Care ministries pastor of Hosanna! Church.

"I found Life Trails to be a God inspired gift and a refreshing break on our road of life. Through what may seem like daily routine, we come to see the mysterious yet miraculous hand of God. I found it encouraging and inspiring as Dave Kranz catches and shares glimpses of the incredible, among what could have been incidental. I have a new appreciation of the beauty of God's creation, life lessons gleaned from the past and a longing for all that lies ahead as together we navigate the journey to our heavenly home."

Tim Murphy—President, Murphy Automotive Inc.

"Dave leans in on his Biology and Earth Science wisdom; mixes in his love of nature and then effectively combines them with Carolyn and his lifelong quest to grow in their relationship with Jesus. He has created page after page of simple life relevant experiences that inspire so vividly that I sensed I was right there with him!" Four words stick with me that are evident throughout the book: "I will be Thankful, I will be Grateful, I will be Prayerful and I will be Humble"

Barb Knudsen—Executive director of teaching and learning for Lakeville Public Schools.

"Dave's collection of beautifully written devotions will cause you to reflect on your journey with Christ. By taking everyday events and people, he shows us how to forge our relationship with God. By sharing his time with Carolyn through cancer, he guides us through their faith-filled journey—an inspiration and path for all who yearn to be closer to God."

Tracey Weaver—Educator and Co-Director of Midwest Volleyball Instructors Camps and Clinics.

"Dave Kranz possesses a unique ability to see God in all of creation and to hear His voice and feel His presence in times of need. His words inspire, bring comfort, encourage, and challenge us to seek God in all circumstances."

For more information contact: Dave Kranz Creations, 17261 Jade Ct, Lakeville, Minnesota 55044. Phone: 952-435–8514. Email: kranzdw1@gmail.com

Cover and DKC logo designed by Dan Kranz.

Cover photo of sunrise taken by Dave Kranz, four hours after his wife's death.

Printed in the United States of America.

Contents

Introduction

In the beginning, God created the heavens. Within this universe there is one star called the Sun. Average in size, not too dangerous, perfect for supporting life. God said, "It is Good." Orbiting this star is a unique planet we call Earth, just the right distance away from the Sun to sustain life. A jigsaw of water and land covers our beautiful home, with an atmosphere that wraps itself around as a protective blanket. Natural cycles dominate, continually renewing the water, land, and air. In a slow but persistent march, the landscape continually changes as tectonics build new land, and weathering turns old rock into soil. Scattered throughout this home, exists an amazing web of life. We are a part of that web, intricately woven in God's image. We enter this world from a watery womb of total dependence, to experience life as a unique creation, one designed to share life with others.

This incredible God loves us so much, He offered His son as our savior. God yet human, powerful yet humble, Jesus came as a servant king. He changed the rules from law to love, by offering himself as a sacrifice for our sin, and promises eternal life with Him in Heaven. Nothing could stop him from completing His mission. Not even death. God the Holy Spirit adds continuity to His promise as an ever-watchful counselor who is, patient, persistent, and powerful. John starts his Gospel stating God has always been here for us. Matthew ends his Gospel with the reassuring words that God will always be here, *even to the end of the age.* This promise and His presence give us hope.

We have been blessed with spiritual gifts to help us interpret God's light, plus mental and physical talents to help us do his work. Together these meld to make us whole. We are his hands and feet, His eyes and heart, we can hear His voice and speak His words to help bring comfort and joy to the people of this Earth. Thank you Lord, because of you, we are blessed, we are loved, we are forgiven, and we are saved.

As you read these devotions may you feel His presence, experience His power, and drink in the peace He offers. You are not alone. God walks by your side as you navigate your life trails.

Life Trails Through God's Creation

Sensing His presence in nature

God has sprinkled excellence all around and wishes for us to notice and appreciate the wonders of Earth. The devotions in this chapter were triggered by observations in nature. To truly appreciate God, it helps to open your senses to the natural world. Imagine the power and creativity it took to create such a dynamic biosphere with its amazing intricacies. We are connected to this natural world, not only as one of its pieces, but also as its designated guardians. May these devotions open your eyes to wonderment and bring you closer to the creator.

Genesis 1:31
"Then God looked over all he had made,
and he saw that it was very good!"

Soaring Above the Soreness

Life can be hard sometimes. Schedules get overfilled, health fails, work becomes an endurance test, or relationships become strained. How do you break out of the doldrums and recapture the luster God intended for you? How about looking for eagles!

Picture a majestic eagle soaring above a mountain stream wings tipped slightly as it banks toward the rising sun. The stream below sparkles against a backdrop of lush vegetation and snowcapped peaks. The eagle calls, announcing "all is well" then catches a thermal, soaring up and out of sight.

This scene exudes a calm peace coupled with the power of hope. What does it take to become like that eagle and soar above the troubles of life? Three things come to mind.

First a soaring eagle appears to float effortlessly through the air when in reality it took a lot of hard work to overcome gravity and gain altitude. What work do you need to do in order to lift yourself up? Second, the eagle relies on updrafts to buoy its flight. We also rely on an updraft—it's called the Holy Spirit. Unlike nature's updrafts, which are variable, the Holy Spirit is available at all times ready to lift you up. Seek His help. Third, like that eagle we need to bank toward "the Son." His light will illuminate our path and help us discover the best route from the pit to the pinnacle. Pick up the Bible and let God speak to you, then reflect on your relationship with Him. Let His peace lift you up and then align yourself with His stream of love. Trust in His power to heal in times of need. Then soar like an eagle with a renewed spirit, anxious to find joy in life.

Isaiah 40:31
"But those who trust in the LORD will find new strength. They will soar high on wings like eagles. They will run and not grow weary. They will walk and not faint."

Beware the Gathering of Vultures

In Luke 17:37 Jesus cites an old proverb to help his disciples interpret the timing of his second coming: *"Just as the gathering of vultures shows there is a carcass nearby, so these signs indicate the end is near."* Jesus is telling them not to pay attention to individual signs but instead pay attention to a number of signs. I would like to propose a parallel analogy.

Vultures are the most visible of the carrion eaters (animals that feed off death). As one vulture circles over a potential meal, others are attracted to join in. This acts as a signal to other scavengers who use the vultures as a beacon for finding dead meat. Once the meal begins, vultures aggressively dig in with their featherless heads, making clean up after the meal an easy task. In most people's minds, these birds are repulsive and ugly.

Have you ever heard the saying "Satan rears his ugly head?" Like the vulture, Satan feeds off death "of the soul". As Satan circles his prey, he too announces a potential feast of sin, which in turn attracts others of like mind. As sin becomes visible, it tends to pull more sin unto itself, thus widening its sphere of influence. Sin often appears to make easy prey out of potentially tough situations and may even taste good to people hungry for earthly delights. Clean up, however, is never easy. Once caught in this trap, sinners become like the vulture – destined to follow the stench of death.

Beware the gathering of vultures. See them for what they are and resist the lure to check out their quarry. Instead choose life, and fly not in circles above death, but soar like an eagle toward the Son of life.

1 Peter 1:14-15
"So you must live as God's obedient children. Don't slip back into your old ways of living to satisfy your own desires. You didn't know any better then. But now you must be holy in everything you do, just as God who chose you is holy."

Lured by the Fog

I woke up this morning to a world covered in fog. The air was calm and everything around me lacked detail with visibility limited to several hundred feet. As I stood wrapped in this blanket of fog, I felt alone but content. My world had shrunk to a size I could handle. I was the center of attention in this world, and the stillness of the wind gave me a sense of comfort. The scene changed dramatically when I got in my car to run an errand. Suddenly the visibility became a danger. While standing still, the fog gave me comfort. Now it created a white-knuckle experience as I drove, unable to see much in front of me. My impressions of the fog were no longer positive. It had deceived me into thinking it could protect me from the outside world. I realized this was only true when I was standing still. Now I couldn't wait for the Sun to burn off the fog and make my path visible again.

In a spiritual sense fog is a tool of the devil. He can convince you of your importance and keep you focused on yourself. When this occurs a false sense of security is built up and the needs of others become invisible. You have become the center of your little world and are forced into inactivity. In this state of mind your talents have little influence, and your contributions to society are minimized. Only the power of God's love can evaporate this fog and allow you to clearly see the path He desires for you.

Don't get lured into the fog of self-centeredness. It will stop you from reaching out, and it will keep you in isolation. Instead, pray for the Son to come out and burn off the fog so you can travel safely under the brilliant light of his love.

Matthew 16:24
"Then Jesus said to his disciples, If any of you wants to be my follower, you must turn from your selfish ways, take up your cross, and follow me."

Road Salt

We were hit by an ice storm last night. When I went outside the sidewalk was as slick as a hockey rink. I was unable to gain any traction. Movement was a jerky, unstable task. Balance was hard to keep, and many muscles were needed to simply move forward. I wished I had some salt to throw down to gain some traction.

This experience made me think about people who have no faith. How do they cope with unexpected problems in their lives? Their lives must resemble a world covered in ice. They slide around expending lots of emotional energy, but don't travel very far toward healing. There is no traction.

I have been blessed with a faith that acts like road salt to get me through times of trial. Two examples come to mind right away. Several years ago my mom died rather unexpectedly. She suffered two stokes within a week and passed away a couple of days later. My faith kept me firmly planted on the ground as friends sprinkled lots of salt on the path in front of me. This prevented me from slipping. Four years later my wife was, as she describes it, given the gift of breast cancer. How could this be considered a gift? Well so many people placed salt on our paths throughout this ordeal that we barely touched the ice below it. Much was learned about the power of faith. God's love for us was clearly evident. She was able to navigate the icy road of surgery, radiation and chemotherapy with a joyful heart.

What allows some people to handle bad situations with a positive outlook while some fall apart? I think it depends on their access to friends and the road salt known as faith. When the next ice storm enters your life I pray you have an ample supply of road salt tucked away in your heart.

Hebrews 10:24
"Let us think of ways to motivate one another
to acts of love and good works."

Worry Free Zone

It has been very dry the past two months. So dry, experts are worried about plants having enough moisture to survive. Guess what? We just received 2.5 inches of rain. God does provide. So why do we tend to worry so much? And what does it do to our life? Proverbs 12:25 reads, *"Worry weighs a person down; an encouraging word cheers a person up."* In reality, by separating us from God, worry is a sin. By washing out the voice of God it tugs at our faith.

We can choose how to react to life situations. A worrywart will allow the negatives to wear down defenses. Like the virus that causes warts, once a stronghold is established it will grow to create a blemish. Or we can be like the optimist who views the glass half full, and search for ways to refill it.

I love the story a friend of mine told about a crowded 747 jet whose flight was cancelled due to mechanical problems. While passengers angrily stood in line waiting for the airline to accommodate their needs, he grabbed a microphone and announced his joy that the problem was discovered on the ground instead of at 30,000 feet. The mood suddenly switched to one of thanks. We can do the same. Be a voice of optimism, and trust in God to send the rain in times of need. Make your life a worry free zone.

Proverbs 12:25
"Worry weighs a person down;
an encouraging word cheers a person up."

The River of Life

Our lives are similar in design to that of a river— always moving, often changing, while flowing toward an ultimate resting place. In our early years life moves fast, seldom slowing down as we tumble over the obstacles set in our path. We easily adjust and look forward to new adventures around each corner. We slow down a bit in mid-life, meandering through the world, searching for answers, enjoying the experiences along the way. In old age we gently move forward at a pace conducive to reflection. Using past experiences, we piece together the world around us, to complete the puzzle of life. Ultimately we move to our final resting place, our work complete.

Along the way new insights are added as tributaries feed us knowledge from a wide range of experiences. Occasionally a dam is placed in front of us, blocking our forward progress. Then there are the times when situations pour in so fast our banks overflow, scattering our life across the floodplain. The good news in this story is found in the riverbed itself. If the bed is strong and well defined, boulders, tributaries, dams and floods cannot stop us from our ultimate resting place. It will direct us, propel us, and ultimately lead us to the ocean of our destiny.

With Christ as the riverbed of your life you need not worry. He will make sure your life flows in the right direction. Momentum will never be a problem, as the Holy Spirit continually showers you with God's love. As life situations change, Christ will help you stay on course. Best of all, He will be waiting with open arms for your arrival in the ocean of eternal joy that we call Heaven.

John 6:40
"For it is my Father's will that all who see his Son and believe in him should have eternal life. I will raise them up at the last day."

I Want to Be Just Like a Tree

Which type of tree do you identify with? The stately pine that always looks green with its top pointed to the sky? Or a broadleaf tree, going through seasonal changes, spreading out into a web of branches? The pine represents a steady life continually focused on God, reaching out from a main trunk to capture His light. The broadleaf represents a life of change. Periods of spiritual growth are followed by mountaintop experiences where God's love is crystal clear shining forth in splendor, then ebbing into valleys of normalcy. Which tree is closest to representing your life?

It doesn't matter which tree your life mimics as long as it is like one of the two. Each grows every year. For every inch of growth skyward there is an inch of growth in the roots. This is what I like most about trees. As a result of root growth they are able to build new branches and new leaves capable of accepting life-giving sunlight. They grow deep to grow strong. Like these trees, we need to strengthen our roots by studying God's word and listening to His desires for our lives. Only then can we grow in faith and reach out to accept His Son's light.

Lord, I want to be like a tree.
Always growing closer to Thee.
Send my roots deep; provide your water:
I want to join you, my heavenly Father.
Feed me, build me, and allow me to grow.
You are my savior, this I know. Amen.

Ephesians 3:16-17
"I pray that from his glorious, unlimited resources he will empower you with inner strength through his Spirit Then Christ will make his home in your hearts as you trust in him. Your roots will grow down into God's love and keep you strong."

Temptation Falls

To most people water doesn't seem like a powerful eroding agent. We play in it, bathe in it and love to sit by it. But it is a force with an amazing ability to wear away even the hardest rock. The Grand Canyon is the most spectacular evidence of its power, but visit any river valley and you can see what the water has accomplished. Within these valleys we are naturally drawn to waterfalls where the sound of rushing water melds with the sight of clear tumbling liquid cascading over a ledge to pound the rocks below. A combination of natural beauty and raw power, these falls are created by layers of soft rock overlaid with a shell of harder rock. Once this upper shell is breached, the soft rock erodes quickly, creating the falls.

Satan works in a similar manner. He continually pelts us with relatively harmless temptations. Over a period of time these combine to erode our spiritual nature. Occasionally sin breaks through our armor creating a deep valley in our soul, which causes a major fall from God.

How do we guard against these temptations? Engineers design concrete dikes entwined with metal mesh to stop rivers from eating away their banks. We can design similar safeguards by laying concrete plans to spend daily time with God. If we entwine this with Christian fellowship and a life emulating Christ, Satan will have a devil of a time puncturing our armor. Like water, temptation flows through our world in an attempt to erode it away. Arm yourself with God's armor and you will reign victorious as temptation falls to defeat.

James 1:14-15
"Temptation comes from our own desires, which entice us and drag us away. These desires give birth to sinful actions. And when sin is allowed to grow, it gives birth to death."

Thunder and Lightning: Not so Frightening

We have experienced several massive thunderstorms in the past week. I used to be afraid of these storms, now I respect their power, but enjoy observing them from the safety of my home. I've witnessed the destructive energy firsthand as a nearby tornado hurled a six-inch tree limb through a picture window as I watched just two feet away. I've been mesmerized by awesome light shows from storms approaching across wilderness lakes, and like most people have been awakened from a sound sleep by claps of thunder. While containing the power to destroy, a thunderstorm's true purpose is to nourish life. They are kind of like good people with bad tempers. If air is lifted slowly, clouds build and rain falls without turbulence. When air is lifted quickly, as in a thunderhead, electrons are stripped from molecules; charges are created, and then BOOM! The electrons streak across the sky trying to neutralize the charge. This lightning bolt superheats the air creating the explosion we call thunder. My early fear came as a result of not understanding these storms while feeling vulnerable to their power. Then I learned how safe we really are inside of our homes. These structures protect us from the wind, rain, and even the lightning. We just need to be smart by staying in the right spots and not straying out into the storm.

In life, God is your home. He creates refuge from the perils that accompany life's storms. When sudden disaster strikes, He is there to comfort. When evil rolls in and clouds your path, He is there to warn and instruct. When stress builds up, He will show you a safe way to discharge it. When the winds of misfortune blow your way, He will instill the courage to see it through. Coupled with these protections is the rain of salvation. He does all of this for those who love Him.

If you are afraid of the storms of life, get to know God by reading His Bible. Start with Psalm 91 then life will never be frightening.

Psalm 91:14
"The LORD says, "I will rescue those who love me.
I will protect those who trust in my name."

Peaceful Purpose

Here I sit on an island in a lake, which is on an island in Lake of the Woods. It is a calm, cloudless morning, and the only sounds are natural. Water gently ripples on the lake as insects skim across its surface: life can be peaceful in the north woods. It makes me realize once again what God meant as he paused at the end of creating this world and said, "It is good."

The journey to this place wasn't quite as peaceful. We spent 12 hours of paddling open water, dragging canoes over beaver dams, wading through bogs, and portaging over land. There were times of sunny calm, overcast breezes and thundershowers. Dry times, wet times, muddy times. Times of rhythmic paddling, coupled with mosquito-infested labor. Why do we do it? What is our goal? For some, it is the challenge and an opportunity to add another patch of experience to the quilt of their life. For others, it's an opportunity to appreciate God's creation from a different perspective.

In life we are continually taking journeys: some pleasant some challenging, some under beautiful conditions, others filled with pitfalls. What is your goal in this journey we call life? Is it just to succeed at each venture? Or is there more? To understand the "more" we need to seek Christ in all we do. His presence will transcend all the earthly components of the journey to provide a peaceful purpose. With Him at your side each journey becomes a joyful experience guided by His love and filled with a peace only God can provide.

Philippians 4:7
*"His peace will guard your hearts and minds
as you live in Christ Jesus."*

Harmony Lake

While on a layover day on a canoe trip in northern Minnesota four people in our group decided to explore by taking a side trip to a tiny unnamed lake near our campsite. Following a small trickle of a stream, we came upon a set of four beaver dams, each with a small pond to paddle across. A beaver lodge guarded the entry to the lake and a loon greeted us with its lonesome call. A granite sided paradise invited us to stay and explore. Tiny sundew graced the shoreline, while vivid red lilies dotted the landscape. The water was teaming with minnows darting between white water lilies hosting numerous colorful insects. We had ventured into a special place where few people had gone before us. This shared experience created a bond between us best expressed by our unofficially naming this place Harmony Lake. We had experienced a beautiful piece of God's creation in a personal way.

Do you plan for side trips in your life? They are well worth it, especially if taken with others. By getting out of your routine and into an adventure you can experience each other in unique ways. Ways where you can feel the wonder and love of God's grace, where you can learn to rely on His guidance as you create a harmonic bond with your traveling companions. God's amazing creation we call Earth is filled with places like Harmony Lake. Yours is waiting to be discovered. Plan to take that side trip and see what God has in store for you.

Psalm 133:1
"How wonderful and pleasant it is
when brothers live together in harmony!"

Rain on Me!

As mountains lift moist air up their slopes there is a cooling that occurs condensing its precious load of water vapor. The resulting rains are the backbone of life. When we allow ours hearts to be lifted by God's spirit, comfort floods our soul to release the precious gifts God has given. This comfort is the backbone of our faith.

Physical rain falls in liquid form. It cleanses and shapes the Earth's surface, helps plants make food, and quenches the thirst of animals. Spiritual rain falls in the form of grace. It cleanses and shapes our soul, nourishes our heart, and quenches our thirst for eternal life.

God truly does want to drench us with love and grace. We only need to ask for it. The limits of who we can become and what we might accomplish are directly related to how high we lift ourselves in His name.

May God's grace shower your life with peace.
May it fill your cup with joy,
And may you blossom with life,
As you continue to serve in His name.

Ask more often —Trust more deeply —Expect more rain.

John 14:12-13
"The truth is, anyone who believes in me will do
the same works I have done, & even greater works,
because I am going to be with the Father.
You can ask for anything in my name, and I will do it."

The Buffer Zone

When canoeing on a big lake with many islands you learn to utilize these islands as buffers. By traveling around the leeward side, zones of rest and protection are created to help you safely reach your destination. Dangerous waves are tamed as they crash into the windward shores expelling their energy on the rocks of the islands. Behind these islands the waves and wind are gentler. An area of calm has been created inviting a period of rest and recuperation. To reach your destination however, you eventually must strike back out into the big water with its wind and waves. The weather is beyond your control, so you must strategically plan the route to compensate for its tantrums. Island hopping is one such strategy.

Life is no different. We are often powerless to control situations surrounding us, so we need to find ways to buffer their onslaught. A relationship with Christ will create islands within the waters of life. He accepts the continual pulse of temptation unto himself, providing a safety zone behind the love of His presence. If we call on Him to join us on our journey of life He will make sure there are plenty of island buffer zones dotting our route. We can't live in these zones our whole life, but as we venture out we are assured the next island is within reach, waiting to regenerate our spirit and strengthen our resolve to finish the journey. Ask Jesus to join you and experience the rejuvenating power of His buffer zones.

Matthew 11:28
"Come to me, all of you who are weary
and carry heavy burdens, and I will give you rest."

Log Jam

We recently visited a friend's cabin. As part of a lake tour we placed small motors on the back of a two canoes and ventured up a swift flowing stream. Unfortunately we were stopped a half-mile into the trip by several trees that had fallen across the water. The following day we returned with a chainsaw in hopes of clearing the path for further exploration. What appeared to be four or five trees turned out to contain much more. Hidden below the surface was a maze of logs tangled and trapped by the current. We pretended to be loggers of old as log after log was freed and floated downstream to our sons who placed them on the banks. As the logjam was dismantled we detected an increase in the stream's current. No longer impeded it was allowed to flow at a natural rate. We returned the next day to explore the upper reaches of the stream.

Occasionally we experience logjams in our personal lives. As we attempt to move forward, they resist growth and if left unattended can become major obstacles. These may be in the form of sinful habits or behaviors that prevent us from being the person God intended. It requires work to free us from these impediments and there is often more to them than meets the eye. You may have to cut out some habits and untangle a few issues, but the effort is worth it. A life free of logjams runs smoothly allowing us to fully explore the life God wants us to experience. Take a few moments to identify your logjams; assemble the tools to dismantle them, and make a plan to accomplish the work. Then enjoy the current of joy created by God's love as your life flows closer to Him.

John 15:2

"He cuts off every branch of mine that doesn't produce fruit,
and he prunes the branches that do bear fruit
so they will produce even more."

Wildfire

Every summer the news is filled with reports of fires that get out of control and burn thousands of acres of forest. If these reach the crowns of the trees, a firestorm of intense heat and destruction roars through the forest engulfing every living thing in its path. These monsters require huge amounts of fuel and rely on dry debris of dead timber on the forest floor. This situation usually exists in mature unmanaged stands of evergreens where winds and old age have toppled trees. Areas like these that have avoided fires for long periods of time are ripe for disaster. If you have ever witnessed the aftermath of a wildfire your first thoughts would include sorrow and disbelief as total destruction of anything green lies before you in a black and sooty landscape. If however you returned to the burn area several years later, you would witness a miraculous renewal of life. Abundant new growth is everywhere and the forest has returned to a healthier state than before the fire.

Life contains its own wildfires: a job suddenly lost, a major illness, or a relationship gone sour. These types of events seem to destroy the "forest" of our life. We become more susceptible to wildfire as the debris of baggage builds up within us. The more we rely on earthly things the worse the fire can become. But know this: No matter how devastated life appears, God promises the hope of re-growth. If He can renew a forest He can certainly help you regain joy and stability in your life. Trust in Him and rely on His help. Believe that God loves you and desires a healthy recovery. Remember the forest is much healthier following the fire— so too are you. Be patient and aim for steady recovery. Someday you will be able to look back and remember the wildfire as you marvel at the beauty that surrounds your new life.

Isaiah 40:29
"He gives power to the weak and strength to the powerless."

Brrrrrrrrrrrr !

It's cold outside, minus 20 degrees to be exact. Life takes on a new dimension when it's this cold. Snow crunches under your feet, cars groan to a start, deep intakes of air hurt, and exposed flesh stings. You don't want to stay out too long. This kind of severe weather is dangerous and requires tools to survive.

First, we make sure to have the proper clothing. By preserving body warmth and preventing penetration of the sub zero temperatures we can spend time in this dangerous environment. We need similar spiritual clothes to survive in this hostile world. By wrapping ourselves in Christ's love, His warmth maintains our internal desire to know Him more, while protecting us from the bite of worldly stings. Second, there are warm retreats where we can function without fear of the cold. God provides spiritual retreats in the form of church communities and close friends. Third, we educate ourselves on survival techniques and act responsibly. The Bible is the ultimate survival guide for this cold world. People who don't prepare for cold weather are in trouble once it comes. The same is true for believers who don't hone their spiritual skills.

When extended periods of cold weather hit we tend to spend too much time in the comfort of our homes allowing cabin fever to infiltrate our lives. This illness is characterized by restlessness coupled with an inward view of life. If cabin fever attacks our spiritual life, we focus too much on the needs of our own church community, forgetting about those who share this earth with us. Jesus commissioned us with these words *"Go and make disciples of all the nations, baptizing them in the name of the Father and the Son and the Holy Spirit."* (Mat 28:19)

I hope everyone has the chance to experience cold weather. It adds to the rich variety this life offers and provides needed tools for survival. Be careful however to protect your heart from losing the heat of Christ's love. Brrrrrrrrrr! Life would be cold if that happened.

Matthew 28:20
"And be sure of this: I am with you always,
even to the end of the age."

23

Windows

Springtime in Minnesota is a time of rebirth and re-acquaintance with the outside world. After a winter of limited sunshine I refocus my life, once again expanding beyond the walls of my home. I find myself looking out windows to appreciate God's creation. However when the sun is just right, a film of winter grime dulls the view and interferes with the peaceful scene beyond. This motivates me to get out the cleaning supplies in hopes of restoring the glass to its original transparency. Glass is an amazing substance. No matter how stained or dirty it becomes, a little elbow grease and the proper cleaner works every time. Now I can enjoy the view as the sun's brilliant light streams unimpeded into our home.

Spring also means Easter is on its way. This is a time of spiritual rebirth and re-acquaintance with the Savior of our world. The Lenten journey guides us inward as we look through the windows of our heart. It is here that God wants us to apply some elbow grease to the grimy film built up from sin and neglect. This desire to clean up our act, coupled with the cleansing grace of Christ's sacrifice, cleans our spiritual windows and restores us to His original design. If we shout Hosanna! (God save us) He will remind us of Good Friday when He did just that. As we look back through the window of time, the image of His love, plus the reality of His power, become crystal clear on Easter morning.

We don't have to wait for spring to clean our windows. He is always willing to shine His brilliant light to fill our hearts with love. Just ask God for his cleanser, (Jesus); apply a little elbow grease, (confession); then open your heart and let his light shine in.

1 John 1:8-9
*"If we claim we have no sin, we are only fooling ourselves and not
living in the truth. But if we confess our sins to him,
he is faithful and just to forgive us our sins
and to cleanse us from all wickedness."*

The Rock

Jesus is described in the Bible as the rock. (Romans 9:33) *"I am placing a stone in Jerusalem that makes people stumble, a rock that makes them fall. But anyone who trusts in him will never be disgraced."* (1 Cor 10:4) *"For they drank from the spiritual rock that traveled with them, and that rock was Christ."*

 I love to walk along the North shore of Lake Superior looking for rocks. Over time these rocks have been tumbled, washed and polished by an endless barrage of water. The result is a vast array of well-rounded, smooth stones. Slowly these rocks will be reduced to sediment and no longer exist. Or will they? Eventually this sediment will be reformed into new rock at the bottom of the lake.

Jesus was like these rocks. He was continually battered by religious leaders, rejected by his hometown, and constantly challenged by Biblical scholars. This resulted in the smoothing of his human nature. It taught him to control his frustration, and temper his sadness when people did not accept his teachings. It strengthened his patience to withstand the barrages of public life. It solidified his resolve to finish the job. How did he do it? The answer lies in his faith, which was rock solid. He trusted in his Father and the importance of his mission. Like the rocks on Lake Superior's shores, he never went away. He was reduced to a criminal in the eyes of his accusers, nailed to the cross to die, but came back to life as our new rock.

This new rock beckons us to follow him. Resist the temptations of this world that try to break you down. Use the trials of life to polish your spirit. Rely on faith to finish your mission. Like rocks, we too will be reduced to sediment. But because of the one true rock's sacrifice, we are invited to join Him in his home for a new life with an eternity of peace.

1 Peter 2:5
"And you are living stones
that God is building into his spiritual temple."

Dammed Up

All too often when faced with major disasters people will shut God out of their life and blame Him for their situation. This is not a good idea. By doing so you create a scenario similar to when a beaver builds a dam across a forest stream. This beautiful area of God's creation is in for a dramatic change. As water builds up behind the dam the surrounding area is flooded creating a desolate forest of dead trees. These trees still have plenty of sunshine to sustain life but their roots have been drowned, which prevents the completion of photosynthesis. Their bare trunks and branches are sentinels of life gone sour. The only hope for restoration in this forest is the destruction of the dam to remove the water. In time the forest will return.

When we dam up God's love by distancing ourselves from Him we are in danger of this same kind of death. By stopping the flow of His peace and comfort a pool of grief builds up around us. His love is still available but the roots of our faith are drowning in layers of self-pity. As God's love pours down on us one essential ingredient to the process of achieving joy is blocked. The Holy Spirit's guiding encouragement is denied entrance. If allowed to continue in these circumstances we are in danger of spiritual death, and we become like that desolate forest in the stagnant beaver pond. Not a joyous sight. To restore joy after a devastating loss, tear down the dam of blame and self-pity, and allow God's stream of love to flow through your life. The pond of grief will disappear, empowering the Holy Spirit to help you recover. It may take time, but eventually the forest of your life will once again be spiritually healthy, restored to its original beauty.

Romans 15:13
"I pray that God, the source of hope, will fill you completely with joy and peace because you trust in him. Then you will overflow with confident hope through the power of the Holy Spirit."

Caught Between Seasons

If you let it, November in the North Country can be depressing. Wedged between seasons, the glorious colors of autumn are gone, the gloom of clouds often fills chilly skies, and winter snows are waiting to fall. It's easy to wonder if the sunny days of summer will ever return.

The mood at this time of year might be similar to that of the disciples after Christ's crucifixion. Life was colorful with Jesus around. Miracles, parables, and travel made each day a new adventure. The "Son's" light daily bathed them in His wonderful glory and there always were plenty of people around to share in the good news. Now he was gone. People scattered, as hope was shattered. They may have wondered if a life of hope would ever return. It must have been pretty depressing. But then an amazing transformation occurred within them. Christ rose from the dead erasing any doubt of who He was. His ministry now made sense to them. Lifted by the power of the Holy Spirit a mighty strength flowed through the apostles creating a small army of ministers. One season of life had ended and an exciting new one had begun, a season of hope, based on love and grace. That season still exists and we are blessed to be living in it. Christ has risen to take our sins away. To top this off, a third season is on the horizon. One so magnificent it is hard to comprehend, an eternity in the presence of God. Bring on the November Blahs! With God in heaven, Jesus in our heart and the Holy Spirit guiding our path, we will prevail to see brighter days!

John 16:22
"You have sorrow now, but I will see you again;
then you will rejoice, and no one can rob you of that joy."

Light up Your Life

Last night I watched a beautiful full moon gracefully slip through a sky dotted with fleeting clouds. Its ever-changing light would glimmer through puffy clumps of water-laden air, then burst forth as a brilliant sphere creating a peaceful flow of serenity.

This experience got me to thinking about the peace sent down to us from God. Like the moon's light, this peace is a reflected energy emanating from a powerful source that is then bounced to Earth in an unending stream by a very special creation, His son Jesus the Christ. Unfortunately this peace is not always felt in its full intensity. Similar to moonlight its varying intensity is not a result of a lessening of the flow, but instead, is a result of earthly interference. You see, the moon is always reflecting light but we aren't always in the correct position to receive it. It is the earth that blocks the light in daytime, while clouds at night sometimes intercede to block it. God's peace is a constant gift from Heaven but earthly situations often keeps it from entering our heart. Maybe it's a fog of indifference, or the mass of scheduled activities that get in the way, or it could be a haze of temptation blocking its path. No matter the cause, it's our reception that determines the volume of peace received. God never stops beaming it toward us.

Ask yourself what parts of your life are dimming the peace God so faithfully shines on your heart, and then clear a path in order to receive it. Look toward His son to soak up this precious gift. Even if you don't see Him clearly, know that, like the moon, God is always there. Remove the earthly blockades and bathe in the glow of His peace. It's sure to light up your life.

Philippians 4:6-7
"Don't worry about anything; instead, pray about everything.
Tell God what you need, and thank him for all he has done.
If you do this, you will experience God's peace, which is far more
wonderful than the human mind can understand."

Sunsets of Faith

Few things in this world can rival the beauty of a sunset. As daylight fades the bright white of its light is filtered to expose the brilliance of its individual parts. First come the magnificent yellows, followed by soft hues of orange. These melt into rich reds, and then slowly fade to the calm of twilight. Not every sunset is like this. If the sky is clear, our sun simply slips below the horizon with the promise of returning the next day. Only on days when clouds fill the horizon, does the sun boldly broadcast its exit for the night. As it approaches the horizon sunlight must travel through more atmosphere to reach the ground. With the scattering powers of particles in the air, various wavelengths are separated from the mix of light to reveal the distinctive colors associated with sunsets.

Our faith has characteristics similar to sunsets. Most days the elements of our faith blend together to light our path in unobtrusive ways. We attend church on Sunday, speak to God in prayer, try to live a moral lifestyle, and so on. Without obstacles these elements create who we are and how we behave in the day-to-day flow of life. Usually these days slip into night without much conscious thought concerning basic faith issues. However, when obstacles jump into our path the true colors of our faith shine forth. First comes our trust in God, which helps us see beyond the current situation, followed by soft murmurs of encouragement heard in prayer. These are bolstered by the comfort of knowing God will stand by us. Finally, the red of Christ's blood sends forgiveness so we may be filled with the calming peace of God. The true colors of faith burst forth to help you enjoy the beauty of life. The next time an obstacle appears in your life, stop to ponder the beauty of your faith and thank our Almighty Father for sunsets.

Hebrews 11:1
"Faith is the confidence that what we hope for will actually happen; it gives us assurance about things we cannot see."

Three Little Pigs – One Big Lesson

Most people are familiar with the story of the three little pigs. The first pig built a house with a minimum of effort. He probably lived life in the moment, seeking only personal pleasure and gain. When the wolf showed up, this pig paid the price. His house offered little resistance to the wolf's attack. The second pig put more effort into building his house, but cut corners and spent only what was needed to get the job done. The wolf had little trouble in toppling this one also. The third pig dedicated all he had to complete his home. He spared no expense and did the job right. This effort paid off. When the wolf came for supper he was unable to break through the protective shell of the house.

Our faith is like those houses. It protects us from sin and acts like a shield against worldly harm. Satan must break through it before he can do his work on you. What type of home have you built? If it's like the first two pigs then beware of troubled times. You might find yourself stripped of your faith and vulnerable to sin and despair. If however you have given your all to build a true relationship with Christ, your faith will withstand anything Satan can throw at you. Imagine the joy the pigs felt as the wolf huffed and puffed on the brick home. They were really safe! If our faith is built of strong material on the solid ground of Christ's love, we too can feel the joy of safety. Ask God to help you design a strong house, then put in the effort to build it right.

Matthew 7:24
"Anyone who listens to my teaching and follows it is wise,
like a person who builds a house on solid rock."

Get Out of Your Rut

During mating season male deer go through a rut. During this time a lot of energy is spent trying to impress females by challenging other males. It's a time of passion when daily tasks and caution take a back seat to the higher goal of continuing the species. These bold behaviors place the deer at personal risk, but allow for an expansion of family beyond its personal lifetime.

There is a more familiar type of rut which is very different from the one described above. It's the rut of familiarity, a deep groove worn into our lives as we routinely perform the daily tasks we think are necessary. This rut leads to complacency and stagnation, two personal attributes that cause a smile to form on the devil's face. He knows the longer we remain in this rut the harder it will be for us to get out of it. While we are there, our focus is inward, allowing opportunities for growth to pass by unnoticed.

God wants us out of the rut and even extends a hand to help us escape. He would like to see us on less traveled roads where new experiences await our arrival. As we move out of the rut our focus moves upward. When we are a little out of our comfort zone we are more willing to rely on Him and less on ourselves. In this environment we are primed for growth and ready for personal breakthroughs. The results are limited only by how big we view our God. If He is a puny God, we are sure to return to the safety of our ruts destined to plod along with the crowd. If, however, he is a powerful God, we are freed to explore life to its fullest, confident in His infinite love and comfortable in His intimate care. We are now ready to step out with a passion for Him, to impact this world in a way that expands His family, leaving a legacy of joy.

Move out of your rut and get into the rut for Jesus Christ. Hang on to Him for an eternal ride filled with adventure and growth.

Psalm 16:11
"You will show me the way of life, granting me the joy of your presence and the pleasures of living with you forever."

Teacher, Teacher, Teacher

There's a little bird that inhabits the northern forest called the ovenbird. Seldom seen but often heard, he sends a resounding "teacher, teacher, teacher" in quick staccato song throughout the day. Bird songs like these remind us of the abundant life inhabiting the forests. As you walk a wooded path, oftentimes the wind rustling the leaves and bird songs are the only auditory addition to the rhythmic beat of your footsteps.

Next time you take such a walk pay attention to these joyful songs expressing the goodness of life. There is a lesson to be learned from the ovenbird and his friends. Their call is to the "Teacher". By calling out to Christ we receive wisdom and are reminded of the joy He brings to our lives. It's similar to the "Hosanna" people shouted as Jesus entered Jerusalem. Christ wants us to call out like the ovenbird breaking the silence to proclaim His name for all to hear. He desires a life of dedicated focus on His love, not to feed His ego or establish dominance, but to provide us with joy. God has an abundance of gifts waiting to be showered upon us. All we need to do is believe and ask for them.

Are you, like the ovenbird, a joyful example of God's beauty whose actions shout "teacher, teacher, teacher" to the world around you? If not, try it, but be prepared for a shower of love. His love acts like the rain in a forest. It will give you the ingredients to grow, transforming your life into one of beauty and joy.

Psalm 98:8
"Let the hills sing out their songs of joy before the Lord."

Are You an Eagle, Or a Chicken?

The image of a chicken is not a good one. Some people are hen pecked, others are called chicken because they are afraid to take chances. If your movements are restricted we say you are cooped up, and nobody really knows why the chicken crossed the road. An eagle however instills a sense of freedom. It is our nation's symbol, it is the epitome of a comeback from endangerment, and is used to convey majestic beauty.

Consider why these two birds are associated with these images. A chicken's world is confined. It is self-focused and protective of its own interests. Easily upset, chickens squawk at the smallest disturbances and stop producing eggs if life isn't just right. Their social structure is status driven and brutal to the underprivileged. Chickens prefer a rigid lifestyle filled with consistency that includes few risks. The eagle, on the other hand, is a wandering hunter who uses thermal updrafts to soar on wings spread wide. Its eyes are constantly taking in the events within its surroundings ready to act at a moments notice. Its voice is purposefully bold, and when an eagle grabs hold of something it doesn't let go.

Which of these descriptions best describes your life? God hopes it is that of the eagle. He admires people who look beyond themselves and scan the horizon in search of ways to serve. He provides the uplifting power of the Holy Spirit to help, as we step out of our comfort zone to do His will. His spirit soars when we spread our wings to utilize the gifts instilled within us. He is quick to communicate when we have our sights on His son, and loves it when we react to His promptings. All angels in heaven sing for joy when we grab onto our faith and speak boldly in His name. You have a choice. Live your life like a chicken, or an eagle. You are an amazing piece of workmanship created by an almighty God. Display yourself in a manner pleasing to Him. Become an Eagle.

Ephesians 2:10
"For we are God's masterpiece. He has created us anew in Christ Jesus, so that we can do the good things he planned for us"

Watched Like a Hawk

Hawks are intriguing animals. Whether perched in a tree or soaring across an open field, they possess a regal image that exudes confidence. They seem to expect success and show extreme patience in achieving it. Sometimes hawks will sit on a branch with a commanding view for hours on end quietly surveying the landscape. At other times they effortlessly glide back and forth on outstretched wings navigating with slight movements of feathers. In both cases their amazing eyes are on constant alert. These eyes don't miss a thing. Even the slightest motion triggers a quick response.

I envision the Holy Spirit working in a similar manner, regal in bearing, constantly alert, and quick to respond. He confidently watches over us like a hawk, patiently waiting to assist at a moment's notice. Like the hawk, the Holy Spirit's response is triggered by motion. This motion is often more spiritual then physical. It is immersed in faith and a relationship with God. By calling out to the Holy Spirit, God's power is unleashed as his spirit soars to our side ready to infiltrate our heart with peace and wisdom.

Paul speaks of this in Romans 8:38 *"And I am convinced that nothing can ever separate us from God's love. Neither death nor life, neither angels nor demons, neither our fears for today nor our worries about tomorrow—not even the powers of hell can separate us from God's love."*

God's patience matches his ability to love. The comfort of knowing He truly cares about us and will respond no matter what, no matter where, brings a peace beyond our comprehension. You see, the Holy Spirit is watching us like a hawk; therefore, we are never more than a heartbeat away from reaching out to receive the love God wishes to give.

Romans 15:13
"I pray that God, the source of hope, will fill you completely with joy and peace because you trust in him. Then you will overflow with confident hope through the power of the Holy Spirit."

Flight Pattern

Here I sit on a quiet night with fireflies dotting the horizon. I am watching a myriad of insects fluttering in a crazed dance around a light. Each bug loops in a frenzied pattern creating random streaks of white to form a maze-like picture. It reminds me of a bunch of children waving sparklers on the Fourth of July. It is amazing that just 20 feet away I feel no bugs. I am not in their flight pattern. They are so focused on the light they detect nothing else.

Unfortunately some of us are like those insects. We streak head long toward the light of Jesus and bathe ourselves in His glow but see nothing else. We get so caught up in our own salvation that our faith becomes "me based". The world passes us by; it is outside of our radar screen. Like the Pharisees, we shine in the glow of public light, yet focus only on our personal salvation.

A few feet to the left of this light is a wrought iron stair rail with several spider webs strung between the posts. These traps are full of unwary insects providing a feast for the web's owner. The devil uses a similar strategy to trap us in his web of lies. The webs created by pride, self service, and ego are sure to ensnare anyone who focuses too much on himself or herself. Jesus reprimanded the Pharisees for falling into these traps and He warns each of us to approach His light with humility. By paying attention to our surroundings and inviting others to join our flight we can avoid the devil's traps, or at least help each other out if we happen to get ensnared.

Next time you see a cloud of insects buzzing around a light ask yourself four simple questions. Am I flying toward the light of God? Is my radar on to detect others? Who might be seeing the light reflected off my actions? Does Jesus approve of my flight pattern?

Philippians 2:3
"Don't be selfish; don't try to impress others.
Be humble, thinking of others as better than yourselves."

Gneiss Job Lord!

Some of the oldest rock in the world can be found near Morton Minnesota. Gneiss (pronounced "nice") formed nearly 3 billion years ago. Large red and black crystals swirl through this granite-like rock telling a tale of its formation. It started as a pool of melted minerals deep in the crust near the beginning of Earth's creation. This pool cooled and crystallized to become granite. A period of extreme heat and pressure changed its original nature into a rock of different characteristics known as Morton gneiss. Because it was buried deep within the Earth it had no chance of ever changing back. Over time the rock on top of it eroded and exposed the gneiss to the powers of weathering on the Earth's surface. Only now that the rock is exposed can its minerals be separated and allowed to continue their cycle. Maybe some day it will be re-melted then cooled to granite once again.

We are like this rock. Changed by societal pressures and the heat of public scrutiny we become someone different from the person God created. We hide our true self and get caught up in the swirling activities of daily life. We in essence bury what we perceive as faults deep inside. These will stay there until we allow our walls to be weathered, bringing to the surface the beauty of His original creation. God weathers us with loving grace. He nudges us into reflection, which leads to confession, forgiveness, and cleansing of our soul. When combined, these act like a huge sponge, which soaks up God's grace, and bathes our hearts with healing. We are wonderfully created in His image. Accept that fact and be sure to thank him for the "gneiss" job done in creating the masterpiece known as you!

Psalm 139:13-14
" You made all the delicate, inner parts of my body
and knit me together in my mother's womb.
Thank you for making me so wonderfully complex!
Your workmanship is marvelous—how well I know it."

Let It Snow

It's snowing outside, the powdery, sparkly type. Just this morning the world looked dirty, a mixture of gray, black and murky white. Now light glistens off a pure white blanket that softens angles and changes contours. A peaceful quiet fills the air making me glad to be alive. As soon as it ends, I don my winter clothes and take off for a walk in a small wooded area behind my house. Looking ahead I see nothing break the smooth white blanket. Behind me is a single set of tracks leading back to my home. A wonderland of dark branches dusted by stark white flakes awaits me. The air is crisp, the sun is bright, and the world is clean. The calm is broken by the call of a chickadee and rabbit tracks trace a path to my right. These sights and sounds remind me all is well. God's beautiful creation has inspired me once again. I return home renewed and refreshed. My head is clear and life is good. I pray that you too have been able to experience moments like these.

This experience has helped me visualize God's grace. When my life gets dirty from sin and my spiritual landscape starts getting dull and drab, I start finding fault with both others and myself. As joy melts away, the dirt shows even more. Not a pretty sight. When I come to my senses and pray for forgiveness, God sends his snow. It washes away the dirt and turns my life back into the worthy wonderland he intended. Peace returns, relationships are restored and life is good. It works every time.

When your life starts drifting down the wrong path, fall on your knees. Talk honestly to God and ask him to "let it snow".

Isaiah 1:18
"Though your sins are like scarlet,
I will make them as white as snow.
Though they are red like crimson,
I will make them as white as wool."

His Rainbow

Did you know that when you see a rainbow it is unique to you? Rainbows are a result of reflected light from water droplets in the air and what you see is a spectrum of colors absorbed by your eyes. God works like that rainbow. He sends his light into the world to be reflected by objects and people in hopes that it will be absorbed and taken to heart. Each of us receives His light in a personal way. We need to sharpen our senses in order to let that light in, so we may become the people God intended. Our ears can detect the hurt and desires of our friends, but they need to be in the listening mode to receive them. Our eyes can see situations occur that shout out for help, but we need to focus in order to interpret them. Our touch is capable of transferring peace and comfort but it needs to make contact to be felt. God's light is being reflected all around us waiting to be received by his people so they may be energized to help others.

Next time you see a rainbow consider the colors. They may have a message for you. Red is at the top of the rainbow to remind us of the importance of Christ's sacrifice. Orange reminds us to be visible and act out our faith. Yellow cautions us against the ever-present temptations of sin. Green reminds us to care for his beautiful creation. Blue symbolizes the cleansing forgiveness of the waters of baptism. When they're put together we see the brilliant white light of salvation and the promise of eternal life in His presence.

May His light shine brightly so you may receive it. Then reflect his light so those around you can also see the beauty of His rainbow.

John 8:12
"I am the light of the world. If you follow me, you won't have to walk in darkness, because you will have the light that leads to life."

Resist the Path of Least Resistance

Rivers, like people have a life cycle. They begin as ribbons of clear water bubbling over an undefined bed, seeking to establish a course. Under the influence of gravity they seek the path of least resistance. Hard rock is bypassed and curves are established as its volume increases creating the power to erode. Over time this process levels the surrounding land as tons of sediment are moved downstream. Near its mouth the river slowly meanders through a flat plain, depositing most of what it picked up along the way.

People who model their lives after a river are heading for trouble. By taking the path of least resistance they become crooked. Each of us started life with clean, pure hearts ready to explore the world, seeking to establish a path. Those who choose the "easy way" by skirting the hard issues lose opportunities to learn and place themselves in the crosshairs of the "keeper of the curve", Satan himself.

Satan loves it when we deviate from our original path and is eager to guide us around the hard parts of life. As we take each curve, things around us erode. Maybe it's a relationship, a moral attitude or Christ-like behavior. Positive attributes are stripped away and our muddied waters end up aimlessly meandering through a flattened valley.

Refocus on the power of God's love and let Him help you tackle the hardships in life. Resist the temptation to take the easy way out and straighten your course. Just as a river's course is straightened when the land is uplifted, your life can straighten out when you lift your heart toward God. He chose not to take the path of least resistance and allowed His Son to go straight to the cross. He awaits you with open arms. Go to Him.

Matthew 26:41
"Keep watch and pray, so that you will not give in to temptation.
For the spirit is willing, but the body is weak!"

The Fruit of Life

Did you know that every fruit was once a flower? Flowering plants rely on the seeds within these fruits to create new life. Fruits come in many forms, acorns, oranges, bananas, maple whirly birds, rose hips, and the grains of wheat are all fruits. Some were bright showy flowers while others were more inconspicuous, but all were flowers. The flower is nature's way of helping pollination occur. Whether it is attracting insects or catching the wind, it is the flower that begins the process of seed making. If a flower is separated from the plant before this process is complete, its purpose in life is diminished. It may give pleasure for a short time in a vase or brighten up the landscape, but its full potential is never reached.

We are like those flowers. God designed us to bloom and instilled individual talents to insure that happens. However, in order to reach our full potential in life, we need to stay attached to our roots. Our roots are the relationship we grow into with Jesus. I have often heard people say you can be a good person and not be connected to Jesus. This is absolutely correct. Millions of non-Christians have had positive effects on humanity, but none were able to move from flower to fruit. As a result, they lost the joy of an eternal new life with Christ. As they flowered good things happened, but without the nourishment of God's love these were short lived. Each flower eventually withers and dies. For non-Christians, the story ends here.

Eternal joy awaits those who do drink in God's love. Their flowers bloom glorious, spreading beauty and love, then a most amazing thing happens. As the petals wither and fall, the new life contained within the flower's womb develops into the seed of everlasting life. You may be a beautiful flower, but are you producing fruit?

John 4:36
*"The harvesters are paid good wages, and the fruit they harvest
is people brought to eternal life. What joy awaits both the planter
and the harvester alike!"*

Color My World

God chose to cover our world with peaceful colors, while the hustle and bustle of mankind is filled with bold colors. Curves dominate the serenity of nature, while straight lines pierce the architecture of human society. That is why we can sit by an ocean for days, or gaze at a forest stream. These are God's refuge from the stress filled world we have created.

Look out at God's glorious creation and feel His calming presence. Blue waves on a beach need energy to keep rolling along— so do we. The pleasing green of spring needs the "sun" to grow— so do we. The colorless breeze that gently keeps trees swaying in rhythmic motion needs high and low pressure systems to sustain them — so do we. The soft hues of a peaceful sunset rely on air — so do we.

Balance these moments with the flashes of intense color that accompany life — the crimson red of emotion, the amber flashes of dangerous moments, the harsh green of envy, and the blackness of sin.

Finally there is the majestic purple of God's royalty and reign over this world. He blends all colors together to create a pure white light — the light of salvation, given as a gift, with no strings attached. Look into the eyes of the people you meet, notice their color and be reminded of the creator who designed this beautiful world.

Psalm 145:5
"I will tell the story of your wonderful goodness;
they will sing with joy of your righteousness."

It's All in the Code

DNA is a double strand of nitrogen bases that determines the physical makeup of who we are. No two people have the same sequence of codes. Therefore we are each unique. Four nitrogen bases, adenine, thymine, cytosine and guanine, make up this extraordinary system. The order in which these bases are arranged determine the production of proteins, which in turn are used to build life. Daily living is also determined by a set of four codes.

Love: **Mark 12:29-31** *"Jesus replied, "The most important commandment is this: 'Listen, O Israel! The LORD our God is the one and only LORD. And you must love the LORD your God with all your heart, all your soul, all your mind, and all your strength.' The second is equally important: 'Love your neighbor as yourself. No other commandment is greater than these."*

Faith: Matthew 7:7-8 *"Keep on asking and you will be given what you ask for. Keep on looking and you will find. Keep on knocking, and the door will be opened. For everyone who asks, receives. Everyone, who seeks, finds."*

Hope: Psalm 16:8-9 *"I know the LORD is always with me. I will not be shaken, for he is right beside me. No wonder my heart is glad, and I rejoice. My body rests in safety."*

Humility: Matthew 23: 11-12 *"The greatest among you must be a servant. But those who exalt themselves will be humbled, and those who humble themselves will be exalted."*

How we arrange these four codes determine our approach to life, which in turn produces peace, joy and salvation. Science has allowed us to understand the code of DNA. The Bible allows us to understand the code of Life. Unlock His mysteries. It's all in the code.

Psalm 119:105
*"Your word is a lamp to guide my feet
and a light for my path."*

Total Comfort

"I look up to the mountains does my help come from there? My help comes from the Lord, who made the heavens and the earth! He will not let you stumble and fall; the one who watches over you will not sleep. Indeed, he who watches over Israel never tires and never sleeps. The Lord himself watches over you! The Lord stands beside you as your protective shade. The sun will not hurt you by day, nor the moon at night. The Lord keeps you from all evil and preserves your life. The Lord keeps watch over you as you come and go, both now and forever."

As I read this passage from Psalm 121, I can't help but feel loved and cared for. I look around and marvel at creation. The creator himself knows me and is my protector. I find comfort in His total care at anytime, in any place, and for any reason. I truly believe this psalm speaks the truth.

Looking back in my life I can see God's vigilance but I wasn't ready to accept it. I was alone and fearful of what people might think of me if I tried new things. I stagnated as life passed me by. At age 30 God led me to a little church called Hosanna! People opened their hearts to me and created a safe haven. God was indeed watching over me and used this church to jump-start my life. His love was discovered. My relationship with God became real and my life changed. I went from being a person locked in the prison of insecurity to a free man secure in the knowledge I am not alone. Alleluia! What a joy it is to have a faithful companion.

Have you found a safe haven where a trust in God can be cultivated? When you do, He will reward you with total comfort.

Psalm 121:8
"The Lord keeps watch over you as you come and go, both now and forever."

Our Greatest Need

A common misconception about the Venus Flytrap is that it eats insects for nourishment. They do indeed trap and dissolve these six-legged creatures, but the flytrap's greatest need is the minerals locked inside the insect bodies. Venus Flytraps have plenty of light to make food, but live in bogs that are too acidic to provide the necessary minerals for healthy growth. Therefore they eat insects for their mineral content.

A common misconception among Jews on Palm Sunday 2,000 years ago was that Jesus rode into Jerusalem to free them from the oppression of Roman rule. They truly believed this was their greatest need. God knew better. Their greatest need, wasn't political, it was spiritual. They needed to be set free from the oppression of sin. Jesus offered them salvation and provided the ingredients of hope, grace, and peace for healthy growth. Unfortunately many did not recognize their greatest need.

What is your greatest need? Are you like those first century Jews looking for a savior who will ride in to solve your earthly needs? Several centuries of oppression had caused frustration to build within the Jewish nation and blinded many to the true nature of Christ's mission. You may also have a history of life's frustrations not meeting your expectations, but don't let that blind you. If you believe your greatest needs are political, monetary, or physical, you are searching for a savior that doesn't exist.

Like the Venus Flytrap we can remain stuck in the bog of life and continually consume opportunities that land in our lap. Or we can admit that our greatest need is fulfilled in Jesus Christ, and allow him to guide us toward a life filled with joy and peace.

John 14:6
"Jesus told him, "I am the way, the truth, and the life.
No one can come to the Father except through me."

Let's Go Fishing

Let's go fishing! For some people these words create an adrenaline rush and set up a seemingly natural set of events. Tackle is assembled, rods stowed, food thrown together, and fishing apparel donned. Then it's off to the lake with boat in tow and friend riding shotgun. Twenty minutes after arriving at the boat landing you are on the water and ready to cast. Life is good as stress melts from your body and oozes out onto the floor of the boat. The world takes a back seat and a bit of sanity is restored to your life.

For Jesus these words have a deeper meaning. He goes fishing for believers. His goal is not to lure us in and hook us for sport; it's to hook us for eternal life. When Jesus hooks someone, the world indeed takes a back seat; sanity is fully restored, and stress melts away. He wraps us in loving arms, and gently returns us to the pond of life, cleansed and renewed. Once caught, our life will never be the same. When the hooks of temptation dangle in front of us He gives us strength to resist nibbling and prevents us from being caught by worldly desires. We experience the joy of freedom and never feel alone. We live our life with the comfort of His care, and the promise of salvation with eternal life.

Has Jesus set his hook in you? If not, bite into His invitation and accept him into your life. If you have been hooked, take some time to fold your hands and say this little prayer. "Dear Lord, let's go fishing!"

Mark 1:16-17
"One day as Jesus was walking along the shore of the Sea of Galilee, he saw Simon and his brother Andrew throwing a net into the water, for they fished for a living. Jesus called out to them, "Come, follow me, and I will show you how to fish for people!"

Thank God for Cabin Times

Life is good, adrenaline is rushing, and a frenzied pack job is in full swing. You are headed to the cabin! The hectic pace of life remains as you escape the city on crowded roads, but that's OK, because the cabin awaits your arrival. Anticipation heightens as traffic thins and familiar landmarks pass by. Finally the cabin is in sight and a transformation begins. Your heart rate slows as thoughts of busy schedules are replaced with memories of quiet times. As you open the door a familiar scent reveals the reality that you have arrived. A calming peace flows from head to toes as stress melts away to make room for simple pleasures. A few chores complete the arrival rituals before you finally step out the front door to relax amidst the essence of a cabin experience. God's beautiful creation; Wow! It just doesn't get better than this.

What is it about a cabin experience that evokes so many positive emotions and vivid memories? First, it is surrounded by God's beauty. Here the majesty and creativity of His work fills your senses with sights, sounds, and smells of the natural world. Second, family and friends are together for chunks of time instead of fragmented interactions embedded in crisscrossing schedules. You have time to enjoy each other's company. Third, the simplicity of cabin life allows for less clutter, less schedule and more relaxation. This naturally opens the lines of communication with God. When combined, these three create an environment that brings you closer to God and heightens the gifts of peace, friendships, and encouragement He so lovingly gives.

Where is your cabin? If it is a place on a lake, treasure it. If it is a designated time at home for friends or family, schedule it. If it's just a few minutes each day where you can place the world on the back burner, make sure it happens. No matter where your cabin time exists, be sure to thank God for the gift of His presence in these times of building relationships with self, family, and our almighty creator.

Luke 2:14
"Glory to God in highest heaven,
and peace on earth to those with whom God is pleased."

Life Is a Roller Coaster Ride – Or Is It?

Life is often characterized as a rollercoaster ride. It contains a lot of ups and downs, loop de loops, and twisty turns. You work hard to reach high points, then suddenly the bottom falls out and down you shoot. The demands of life can make your head spin as life changes create bends in your path. This ride can be exciting and keeps you energized, but it has one major flaw. It ends in the same place it started because roller coasters are man-made. If you pattern your life after man-made creations, that's exactly where you will end up – right where you started.

It may be better to characterize life as a mountain climbing experience. It still has the same features, but a better ending. As a climber approaches the mountain, he ascends many small peaks and descends into numerous valleys, each one a little bit higher than the last. He winds his way around obstacles and has many decisions to make in choosing a route. Sometimes the going is rough and he needs to rope in for protection as he picks his way up one step at a time. At other times it's an easy hike on an obvious path. This experience isn't flawed because it ends in a higher place created by God – the summit.

God created each particle of this mountain and invites us to explore. You will have to work to climb the peaks but the view makes the effort worth it. Each valley brings a new peak into view to encourage you onward. When you come to hard times and the climb becomes difficult, He offers you protection against falls. He also provides a detailed guidebook to help you navigate.

You can ride the rollercoaster by yourself, but you should never mountain climb alone. So ask God to join you in the adventure of a lifetime and explore His creation we call "life". I hear the view at the summit is awesome!

Psalm 24:3-4
"Who may climb the mountain of the Lord? Who may stand in his holy place? Only those whose hands and hearts are pure."

I Believe

The monarch butterfly has an amazing life story. It starts as a tiny egg on a milkweed plant and then hatches into a colorful caterpillar that spends its time feeding on succulent leaves. If its life story ended here on the milkweed, winter would descend and freeze the caterpillar's body ending any hope of a new life. But before winter reaches out its icy claws, a miracle happens. The caterpillar changes into a chrysalis then transforms to the beautiful orange and black winged butterfly we see flitting around our yards in the fall. A seemingly impossible task now awaits this delicate creature. In order to cheat winter's grasp it must fly thousands of miles to a safe haven in Mexico. Imagine the scope of this migration!

We also face a migration of immense scope that is hard to comprehend yet necessary for our life cycle to complete its intended course. Our destination is heaven. If we stay as caterpillars and feed on the fruits of this world we will be able to grow and stay alive but the icy grip of death will eventually come to take us away. If, however, we feed on the Word of God and simply believe in the miracle of his salvation, we will be transformed into the beautiful creatures of God's original intentions, uniquely created in his image. As believers we are given the tools to fly toward our ultimate destination. Here we are invited to spend eternity with the One who made us. The choice is yours: crawl around this world and feed on its flashy but shallow offerings, or choose to feast on the Word of God and experience the thrill of flight to the safest of all havens. Simply believe and receive.

Galatians 3:22
"But the Scriptures declare that we are all prisoners of sin,
so we receive God's promise of freedom
only by believing in Jesus Christ."

Hurricanes

It starts with a build-up of energy near the equator. Air cascades upward in a violent spiral searching for escape in a mountainous cloudbank. It carries with it an enormous volume of water vapor extracted from the ocean below. Pressure drops and pulls in the neighboring air to reinforce the growing power of this storm. A hurricane is born. Slowly it moves journeying northward to devour whatever crosses its path. Warm water from below and heat from the sun above feed its energy, sustaining its fury. The hurricane marches unabated until deprived of this energy source. Then it is slowly doused as friction and rainfall drain the energy from its grasp. For those in its path, it is hard to find anything positive in this scenario, but it is there. The release of energy is vital to the health of our atmosphere and the rainfall important in filling water tables. Life will come back. It's part of God's design.

Sometimes a storm enters our lives like a hurricane. It may be from physical damage due to weather, disease, or accident. It may be related to relationships, jobs, or mental health. No matter the cause, these devastating events blow through our lives leaving a path of pain and destruction. But life will come back. It's part of God's promise. At times like this, the winds of the Holy Spirit swirl His protection around you to bring hope and guidance. This allows you to become like the eye of the storm drawing help and compassion from family and friends. The life giving water of Christ's love rains down, drenching you with a peace that only He can give. Life starts anew. It will never be the same, but it might be healthier than before, simply because you weathered the storm.

In stormy times accept the love that surrounds you and draw on the hope that life will be refreshed. After all, like a hurricane, you are an important part of God's design.

Psalm 59:16
"But as for me, I will sing about your power.
Each morning I will sing with joy about your unfailing love."

Life Trails With Our Lord

Walking with Him through everyday life

Matthew 28:20
"And be sure of this:
I am with you always, even to the end of the age."

In relation to God — That says it all.

May these devotions help you get closer to Jesus, who desires a relationship with you more than anything else in this world.

God wants us to have relationships with people. Many of life's pathways are filled with the presence of others. Together we walk the trails, and experience the trials of life. We need each other to love with, to laugh with, to cry with, and to learn with.

May these devotions help remind you of the important roles people play in your life; show you the value of having a small group, and underscore the love of God that shines through the beauty of people.

Matthew 18:20
"For where two or three gather
together as my followers,
I am there among them."

The Perfect Shepherd

The following narration might be that of a sheep.
Read it from the sheep's perspective.

"Humans—they are all so different, some can be trusted some not. Some work hard to care for me, others are lazy and could care less about my safety. My favorite shepherd is the one who finds lush green pastures for us to feed. Just when I am full, he leads me to fresh water. I rest peacefully when he is guarding me. Though wolves lurk in the shadows, they are fearful of his power, and stay away. I fear nothing when he is near, not even when we are led through treacherous terrain where footing is unstable and predators abundant. His love and diligence comfort me. I know if I falter he will help. I may be a helpless sheep but with him I feel like a king. I am offered the best this world can provide. I live with pride and feel fully loved. I wish I could dwell in his flock forever."

Wouldn't it be great if we as humans could speak as highly of a leader as this sheep does? His shepherd sounds perfect. He is always on the watch, ready to help while providing the necessities of life. He is a fierce protector able to defeat all foes. No wonder this sheep wants to live in his flock forever.

Come to think of it we do have a leader like this His name is Jesus and He wants us all to join His flock. Does this sound too good to be true? Christ is often depicted as a shepherd and we as his sheep. Read Psalm 23, and praise God for providing us with the perfect Shepherd.

Psalm 23:1
"The LORD is my shepherd;
I have all that I need."

The Serenity of Surrender

A warm sunny day with a light breeze whispering through a pine forest refreshes your spirit as you gaze out at a majestic waterfall. A quiet evening with a small group of friends, sharing stories as soft music whispers through a candle lit room. Returning home from work on a Friday afternoon carrying an empty to-do list, knowing you used your God-given talents to their fullest potential. Standing around a warm campfire discussing life as it relates to God's word. Contemplating the awesome gift of the Christ child whose purpose in life was to save us from sin.

Moments like these are in stark contrast to the all too familiar scene that follows. Stress and aggravation mount as you fight a losing battle to clear your schedule in order to spend time with Jesus. It just doesn't seem to be working. You have too much to do, too many things to accomplish, and too many people counting on you.

What makes this scenario different from the first examples? It's self-focused. Appreciating God's creation, sharing in a small group, giving credit to God for jobs well done, and being thankful for the gift of salvation all indicate a surrender of self. It's not about you. Through this surrender we gain a powerful ally and all of His resources. We have a friend for life with an arsenal of tools designed to fill our heart with peace, and our life with joy. He surrounds us with a beautiful world while placing friends within it to share our victories and defeats. He helps us discover our talents while providing avenues to utilize them. In turn we learn to praise His name as we accept the invitation to join His family. Surprisingly, holes appear in our schedule, begging to be filled with the joy of His presence. Surrender to God, and experience the peaceful serenity only He can provide.

It's not about you. It's not about me.
It's about God working through thee.

Colossians 1:9
"We ask God to give you complete knowledge of his will and to give you spiritual wisdom and understanding."

Three Dimensions

To fully appreciate our world with any depth, you need to take in all three dimensions of its physical nature. To look only at height is to see lines. Lines can define things but there is a lot of empty space between them. Add width to this view and you can fill in the area between the lines, but it is still flat. Only when depth is added can objects be fully defined and their true nature discovered.

To fully appreciate God's love for us, our perception of him also needs to be three-dimensional. To view God only as the creator allows us to be awed by the splendor of the natural world and our role within it. There is much beauty in this scene and it helps us understand the magnitude of his power. That's not the whole picture however. Add Jesus and we see how important our salvation is to God. He sacrificed his only son to prove once and for all we are worthy of his love. The full depth of God's love isn't realized until we add His third dimension, the Holy Spirit. With His guidance and continued presence we are able to withstand temptation while living life to our fullest potential. Three in one—Father, Son, and Holy Spirit. Together they make our world a place of wonder and hope, filled with beauty and companionship. We can feel loved and protected by a God of three dimensions.

Next time you pray, thank God for his creation, ask Jesus for his forgiveness, and invite the Holy Spirit to guide your path. Then set out into the world armed to appreciate it in the fullness of His three dimensions

Psalm 46:1-2
"God is our refuge and strength,
always ready to help in times of trouble.
So we will not fear."

The Light of the World

Christ is often referred to as the light of the world. Have you ever wondered where light comes from and its importance in our lives? Much of what we experience is carried by light to our eyes and then transferred to brain waves for interpretation. Each photon of light is a result of an electron absorbing energy and jumping to a new orbit around its nucleus. An instant later it returns to its original orbit and emits the absorbed energy as light.

Christ's light isn't a visible ray of energy. Instead, it's an energy based on love. Jesus absorbed his father's love, using this to jump to a new home here on Earth. His entire ministry orbited around the nucleus of his message. Then Christ returned to his original home but not before emitting the light of His love in one glorious sacrifice. When Jesus died on the cross he transferred God's love to an ever-widening beam of grace that shines for eternity. This light is *felt* more than seen, *experienced* more than interpreted. It's a light that is fully rechargeable and always shining.

We are free to use this light whenever we need it. When your path becomes shaded by poor decisions, that light can turn shadows into sunshine. When temptation lures you astray, that light can destroy the deceiver. When disaster strikes, that light can turn desperation into inspiration. When life loses meaning, that light can turn passivity into purpose. When life ends, that light can turn damnation into delight. That light is Jesus the Christ. It shines for eternity and cannot be put out. He wants to shine it on you. So light up your world by saying, "yes" to the light of the World.

John 8: 12

"I am the light of the world. If you follow me, you won't have to walk in darkness, because you will have the light that leads to life."

Stability

Life is held together by atomic attractions called bonds. One type of these bonds, known as *covalent*, is the result of elements sharing electrons. Electrons orbit in specific energy shells around the nucleus of an atom. The outermost orbit is crucial to the stability of that atom. If it is full, stability ensues. If not, the atom is unstable and becomes chemically active to seek stability. When two elements share electrons each can become stable and the *covalent* bond is formed. By orbiting both elements, these electrons help bind the atoms together to form a compound. The miracle of this bonding is seen in the results. The new compound is not only stable but also different than the elements making it up.

Our stability can also be increased through bonding. When you ask God to share his love with you, He orbits your life and makes a connection between himself and your heart. Just like the elements that bond to form compounds, you become a new creation. The characteristics within you meld to the love of God. Suddenly life becomes more stable. Hardships remain, but they become easier to deflect and joy is more abundant. You interact with others in a new way, a way that is grounded in love.

Another thing about compounds in nature is that they combine with others to create molecules that in turn connect to form the complex substances of life. This new you is also designed to interact with others. By further bonding with a small group and a church community you become an important part of God's plan we call Christian living.

You have a choice. Struggle through the chemistry of life by yourself and constantly search for stability, or share your life with God and His people. Allow His love to interact with yours so you can become the full creation he intended in the first place.

2 Corinthians 5:17
"This means that anyone who belongs to Christ has become a new person. The old life is gone; a new life has begun!"

In the Name of the Father, Son, and Holy Spirit

A rewriting of Psalm 136

Dear almighty God: I give you praise,
My voice and love to you I raise.
Creator of Earth and all that is good,
Hear my prayer as only you could.
I lift my heart to you oh Lord,
I request your presence and your word.

Blessed Jesus show me the way,
I invite you in for an eternal stay.
You, who came so I might live,
Guide my path so I may give.
Reveal your word,
Bring out what is true,
And help me Lord get closer to you.
I lift my heart to you oh Lord,
Wrap me up in your loving cord.

Fill my spirit with joy and peace,
Let your power be released.
Melt the walls that seek to separate,
Free my tongue as I communicate.
I lift my heart to you oh Lord,
Help me stand with your righteous sword.

I lift my heart to you oh Lord,
In praise and in thanksgiving.
I lift my heart to you oh Lord,
And say thank you for giving. Amen

May the peace and joy of Christ's love bathe you in its
warmth, to lift your spirits and lighten your load.

Psalm 136:1
"Give thanks to the Lord, for he is good!
His faithful love endures forever."

Baked to Perfection

I love eating chocolate chip cookie dough. Those soft lumps of sweetness with hard chocolate nuggets create a distinct taste sensation. Cookie dough is not a finished product however, and is no match for a slightly warm chocolate chip cookie. With a crisp golden brown shell and gooey chocolate innards, this melt in your mouth delight is unmatched. What a treat!

People who have accepted Christ have experienced the same transformation. They have developed into the wonderful being God intended. Prior to this acceptance they may have been good people but like cookie dough they lacked a definite moral shape and were easily molded by earthly desires. They also lacked a protective coat and were easily wounded by the hardships of life. Their heart was sweet but hard to open. Once they basked in the glow of Christ's love a change took place. The physical ingredients were the same but the product was new. Their heart softened and opened itself up to the loving grace of our father. Their spiritual armor solidified allowing them to defend their beliefs and deflect the hurts hurled by society. They became whole and realized they are loved.

Are you still cookie dough? Or have you allowed God's love to transform you? Place yourself in His warm presence and allow Him to bake you to perfection. Then share yourself with others, for you have become one of God's sweet treats.

Revelations 21:5
"And the one sitting on the throne said,
"Look, I am making everything new!"

CPR

When someone's heart fails, doctors quickly administer CPR to resuscitate the patient. This procedure has saved many lives over the years. God has been performing this procedure for over 2000 years. He sent his son to resuscitate the hearts of all believers and then asked the Holy Spirit to patrol Earth for all subsequent emergencies of the heart. Unlike the medical profession, God doesn't send us a bill for services rendered. Instead He sends the gifts of grace and eternal life. A heart electrified by Christ's love is stronger. It is now filled with three chargers that will help us stay close to Him:

Courage to come clean, like the prodigal son (Luke 15): As we admit sins and ask for forgiveness we experience the peace of acceptance by our Father. This gives us the strength to speak for Christ.

Persistence to never let up and always get up: Through daily devotions and a constant eye on the path of righteousness we are strengthened by dependence on Him. God is there to pick us up whenever we stumble.

Real relationships with Christ and our fellow humans: Friends stay in contact and share their innermost thoughts. Jesus listens. Jesus cares. Call His name and He'll be there. The same is true of small groups. These relationships go beyond the surface to the heart of matters.

Does your heart need some CPR? If so, call out to God and a few friends. Any heart can be mended and then filled with joy. The process is simple. Ask for forgiveness and thank Him for saving you. Accept Christ into your life, and join a small group for continued support. Please don't delay—you never know when you may need medical CPR.

1 John 1:9
"if we confess our sins to him, he is faithful and just to forgive us our sins and to cleanse us from all wickedness."

Downshifting

Remember the Simon and Garfunkel song " Slow down you're moving too fast, you got to make the morning last. Just kicking down the cobblestones looking for love and feeling groovy"? When was the last time you truly slowed down, looked for God's love, and felt his presence?

Continually running in overdrive stresses our engine. It prevents us from enjoying the scenery and narrows our focus on life. When we downshift to spend time with Jesus, and look upward, a connection is established. He is ready to remind us of our importance to Him, and will help us navigate life. As children of God we are constantly bathed in love. No matter how much we neglect Him or ourselves, we are welcomed with open arms to his spa for a free bath, and massage. That's where He cleanses our soul and fills our spiritual tanks. With clean windows and plenty of fuel, we can reenter the autobahn of life knowing we are loved. Now we are ready for unexpected potholes and excited about the journey ahead. It's time to shift into overdrive with purpose and pleasure.

Plan some daily downshifting. As Psalm 46:1 says *"God is our refuge and strength, always ready to help in times of trouble."* If you are moving too fast you might miss the turnoff to His refuge. So slow down and turn to Him.

Psalm 46:10
"Be still, and know that I am God!"

Pilot Light

I recently installed a gas fireplace in our family room. With a simple flick of a switch we can relax and watch the flames dance among the logs. Warmth from the fire fills the room wrapping us in its comfort. This scene can be repeated at will due to a small flame called a pilot light, which stays lit, always ready to ignite the full fire.

So what is our pilot light and how do we keep it lit? By staying in touch with God. Each time we pray, worship, or read God's Word, we feed our pilot light. It starts with personal praise and prayer. Our times with God, whether scheduled or spur of the moment, keep the relationship strong and invite the Holy Spirit to check our fuel level. Regular worship and small group experiences maintain the fuel lines and prevent rust from clogging the jets. Education and reading God's instruction book give us knowledge to properly monitor and adjust the equipment. Together, these activities keep our pilot light burning steadily, so when an opportunity to minister comes our way we can flip on the switch and spread God's holy fire through our actions. When this happens, people come to know the marvel of God's light and experience the warmth of His love. Are you maintaining your pilot light?

John 15:5
"Yes, I am the vine; you are the branches.
Those who remain in me, and I in them, will produce much fruit.
For apart from me you can do nothing."

A Delightful Delay

I recently learned a lesson on the value of waiting. My hobby is woodworking. I enjoy creating pieces with my band saw incorporating Christian symbolism intended as gifts for the home. I had mailed a package of these items to a friend, but the package was returned, "address unknown". Fortunately, I had put my return address on the original package. Otherwise it would have ended up in a warehouse waiting for no one to pick it up. I fixed the address and was returning to the post office to mail the package a second time when an inspiration hit me. I turned around and went home to create a new piece that was perfectly suited for this particular friend. The Lord had used this delay for good. My disappointment when the original package returned was transformed to wonderment that allowed me to create the perfect gift.

I realized life is like that package. No matter what happens to us, we can be assured of being delivered. We can take great comfort in knowing our return address in heaven will never change. Rather than getting frustrated when things don't go the way you plan and a delay occurs, turn to God for guidance. Maybe he has even better things in mind for the situation. Maintain your relationship with Him so you are assured of your eternal address.

Psalm 16:11
"You will show me the way of life, granting me the joy of your presence and the pleasures of living with you forever."

Stretch Me Lord

Like elastic, we are designed to stretch in order to fit current life situations. The problem is that we, like elastic, tend to favor the retracted form. As a result we often get too comfortable and have a tendency to let life get stale. Here is a prayer that might help you stretch out.

Lord I feel small and insignificant. Am I worthy to see myself in any other way? I ask myself, "Why am I special in your eyes?" I am a mere mortal who has fallen short of your glory. I am but a speck in your creation, yet you want me to leave my mark. Lord, help me to feel your love. Open my eyes so I may view the gifts you placed within me. Nourish my heart so it may spread your love throughout my body. Ignite my brain with the wisdom of your words so I may feel whole and wonderful in your sight. Then set me free, confident in using your gifts. Humble, yet proud of whose I am. Lead me to the waters of your loving grace so I may be cleansed of sin. Wash away all thoughts of unworthiness. You crowned me with glory and honor to be a shepherd of your creation. Fill me with your Holy Spirit and strengthen my heart, so I may boldly go forth to accomplish the deeds you desire.

Thank you Lord, for creating me…
Help me see what I can be.
I understand that you are key,
So let my life be stretched by thee.
Amen.

Psalm 8:1
"O LORD, our Lord, your majestic name fills the earth!"

Asleep in the Light

For some people sleeping during daylight hours is normal. Most of us would call this a nap. Every day around 3:00 PM my biological clock tells me its naptime. If I give in to this urge I usually wake up groggy and disoriented, only to gain a second wind around bedtime. The urge to nap is strong, but I know I am better off without it. The best remedy is to engage in physical activity that recharges my body and gets me over the urge to sleep.

The world around us continually beckons us to take spiritual naps. By shutting down our soul these naps allow us to keep our feet in the church, while our eyes focus on the world. In this state of mind, our spirit is numbed, as sin slowly takes hold. If allowed to continue, the world becomes our norm, as God slips into the recesses of our mind. Thankfully we usually wake up from these spiritual naps, albeit disoriented, wondering how we allowed ourselves to slip away from God. The good news in this scenario involves our Savior Jesus Christ and the devil himself, who constantly tries to lull us into spiritual naps. He continually places temptations in front of our eyes with the hope of convincing us to give in to them. Thankfully the devil is no match for Jesus. All we need do is refocus on Him and engage in some spiritual activity. He guarantees victory and grants us a second wind, which rejuvenates our spirit and sends the devil in retreat.

Are you asleep in the light? If so, pull away the shades of Earthly desires and let His light shine upon your soul. As you absorb His love the joy of His presence will reawaken your life.

1 Corinthians 10:13
" And God is faithful. He will not allow the temptation to be more than you can stand. When you are tempted, he will show you a way out so that you can endure."

Sailing Through Life

Lake Pepin is a mile wide stretch of the Mississippi River in southeastern Minnesota. Rimmed by 400-foot bluffs, this picturesque setting is home to many sailboats. Whether bobbing in the harbor or skimming across the lake, these boats exude a peaceful aura. While moored in the harbor winds gently rock these majestic craft, but pass by with little effect on them. If you hoist the sail, the situation drastically changes. Held by a solid mast, the sail billows as it fills with wind, propelling the craft forward. By adjusting the sail and controlling the rudder the captain can successfully navigate the lake and capture the power of the wind.

If we are to be captains of our lives and wish to navigate the waters ahead of us, we can learn from these sailboats. First, a strong mast must be firmly secured to our hull. The Bible is top of the line in this category. It can withstand the strongest gales life can dish out. Its enduring strength is legendary with versatility matched by none. Next we need a sail capable of catching the wind. I recommend the faith brand. With faith we are assured of gaining maximum power and consistent performance. Finally we need a rudder. For 2000 years Jesus Christ has outperformed all others and comes with an eternal guarantee.

Before setting out on your next journey, check the condition of the equipment on your boat then hoist your sail to capture the power of the Holy Spirit. With Christ as your rudder and the Bible holding up your faith, your journey will be filled with the joy of sailing among the beautiful waters of Gods creation.

John 14:16-17
"And I will ask the Father, and he will give you
another Advocate, who will never leave you.
He is the Holy Spirit, who leads into all truth."

Shower Time

Few things in life are more refreshing than a shower. Whether it's a cool gentle flow following a workout, or a hot pounding blast that wakes you up in the morning, showers are a gift of cleanliness and revitalization. When coupled with soap, water has an amazing ability to clean nearly anything off your skin. The constant pitter-patter of droplets stimulates nerve cells and reawakens your senses. You may enter dirty and tired, but leave clean and refreshed. Daily showers are a routine for many of us, but spiritual showers are not.

Confession has the same effect on our soul as showers have on our body. It cleanses our spirit as the guilt and grime of daily temptations are flushed away. Our relationship with God is stimulated as His love washes over us. Instead of soap and water, God uses an even more powerful cleanser forgiveness. Combined with His love, it is able to wash away all things unclean. If you go several days without showering, a grubby feeling sticks to your body. The same is true of confession. As sin builds up it coats your soul and prevents joy from reaching the surface. You feel dirty and life is no longer fresh.

So add a shower of confession to your daily routine. God never runs low on love and His forgiveness is always ready to flow. All you need do is turn on His faucet and receive the cleansing stream of His precious gift. Is it shower time?

Proverbs 28:13
"People who conceal their sins will not prosper, but if they confess and turn from them, they will receive mercy"

Thanks for Giving

I thank you Lord for the gift of living.
Its precious nature keeps on giving,
And afterwards we'll join together,
Enjoying life forever and ever.

I thank you Lord for the gift of light.
Your path and guidance are so right.
I praise you for its beams so bright,
Darkness shattered – no more night.

I thank you Lord for the gift of listening.
As I repent my soul starts glistening.
You know my heart; I know your voice,
I'm eternally grateful I made the choice.

I thank you lord for the gift of love.
I feel it often through your spiritual dove.
A love so deep, if I were the only one,
Still you would have sent your only son.

I have so much to be thankful for,
I am so glad you knocked on my door.
Light and listening, love and living,
But most of all, thanks for giving!

We all have so much to be thankful for. So often we get caught up in what we don't have, or what our neighbors do have, that we forget. If we spend more time each day giving thanks for the blessings in our life and less time looking at what others have, our perception of life turns from almost empty, to nearly full. God wants to fill our life with joy. Ask for it, accept it, and always remember to say, "Thanks for giving".

Psalm 118:1
"Give thanks to the Lord, for he is good!
His faithful love endures forever."

Freeway Travel

The smoothest way to travel long distances in your car is to drive the freeways. These roads are designed with wide shoulders and lane separations to increase safety at high speeds. Traffic flow is improved by: a lack of intersections with stop signs, consistent speed limits, small slopes with low grades, broad right of ways, and gentle curves to enhance visibility. Add too many vehicles however, and even the best-designed roads become frustrating ribbons of accidents waiting to happen. Factor in poor driving habits, and freeways lose most of what they were designed to accomplish.

Christianity has a few parallels. The Bible contains rules and regulations designed to insure our safety. Christ paved a path for us to follow and sent the Holy Spirit to light the way. When we know the rules and travel with the spirit, life's flow is improved. A relationship with Jesus removes many sinful stop signs. Visibility is improved as we allow the light of God's love into our heart. Safety for eternity is assured by accepting Christ as our savior.

Life as a Christian would be easy if there weren't so many worldly vehicles in our path. Alas, Satan travels the same roads with his many tempting friends. When your freeway is crowded make sure your personal living habits promote spiritual safety. Rely on Christ's peace to keep you calm, and keep moving forward.

Unlike our freeway system, a life with Jesus never breaks down. There are no guarantees the speed limit will be maintained, but safety is assured. So as you travel the freeways of life, be sure to thank the Creator for the safety of His roads.

1 Corinthians 2:9
"No eye has seen, no ear has heard, and no mind has imagined what God has prepared for those who love him."

Slow Me Down, Lord

Expanded from **Slow me down, Lord**. Author unknown

Slow me down, Lord. — Ease the pounding of my heart by the quieting of my soul. Steady my hurried pace with a vision of the eternal reach of time. Give me, amid the confusion of the day, the calmness of the everlasting hills.

Break the tensions of my nerves and muscles with the soothing music of the singing streams that live in my memory. Help me to know the magical, restoring power of sleep.

Teach me the art of taking minute vacations – of slowing down to look at a flower, to chat with a friend, to pet a dog, to read a few lines from a good book.

Slow me down, Lord. — Inspire me to send my roots deep into the soil of life's enduring values that I may grow toward the stars of my greater destiny.

Send your light upon me, so I may follow your path. Guide me with your spirit and light the fires of my soul. Humble me so I may accept your will and go forward with a servant's heart. Strengthen me—give me the courage to expand.

Slow me down, Lord. — I want to know your peace. Help me seek your presence and hear your voice. Remove the clutter of this world so I may clear my mind. I desire to feel your love.

Slow me down, Lord. —Slow me down.

John 14:27
"I am leaving you with a gift—peace of mind and heart. And the peace I give is a gift the world cannot give.
So don't be troubled or afraid."

Whose Trophy Are You?

If there is a fence that separates, good from evil, the Devil owns that fence. People who sit on it look good and go through the motions of being upstanding citizens. These people don't participate in major forms of sinful behaviors, and if asked would call themselves contributors to society. Sadly many of these people are spiritually dead and are on display as Satan's trophies. By keeping us on the fence, Satan is able to neutralize our potential without damaging our social image.

How does Satan keep us on the fence? The first chapter of Judges gives some insight through a story of man who became such a trophy. Judah routed the Canaanites and captured their king (Adoni-Bezek). Instead of killing him, they kept the king alive, but rendered him harmless by cutting off his thumbs and big toes. Without thumbs Adoni-Bezek was unable to wield a sword or defend himself with a shield. Without big toes he was unable to run or maintain balance. He had become a helpless symbol of defeat placed on display for all to see.

Missing fingers and toes are not easily visible, yet they are capable of disabling the whole person. Satan can grab hold of a few small areas of our life and turn us into his trophies. We are unable to become the full creation God intended. The good news is this. Unlike Adoni-Bezek, we need not be crippled for life. Jesus saw to that when he became God's ultimate trophy. God did not place Jesus on a fence. He placed him on a cross in the center of a field of mercy and invites you to get off the fence to follow His son. If we surrender our faults to God and try to change our ways, He promises to heal us. Fully restored, we may once again live life to the fullness God intended. By not straddling the fence, we can run free to capture the joy of life.

Malachi 4:2
"But for you who fear my name, the Son of Righteousness will rise with healing in his wings. And you will go free, leaping with joy like calves let out to pasture."

Pivot Point

In basketball one of the first skills you are taught is the pivot. By planting one foot and rotating on it, you can change direction to gain an advantage on your defender. The pivotal point in a game or political campaign is the specific action that helped decide the outcome of that contest. Life is full of pivotal events such as these, which become instrumental in determining the direction of our lives.

There's a story of a ship whose captain notices a brilliant light shining directly off the bow. The captain radioed an order for the object radiating this beam of light to change course because he was not about to. After several challenges back and forth, the ship captain sent this message: "I am the captain of a destroyer. You must change course." The reply came back, "I am a lighthouse. You must change course." Immediately the captain made a decision to pivot his ship. Originally he was making a choice based on his own desires without knowing the full story. If he had stayed on this course his ship would have smashed into the rocks reaping destruction to all under his care.

When we come to pivotal points in our lives we have two choices: make the decision based on what we want; or listen to God, the lighthouse of our life. Would a basketball player pivot left just because he wants to? Should politicians make decisions based solely on personal desires? I hope not. Similarly, when life presents pivotal moments, we need to make decisions based on a consultation with our lighthouse. God desires to spread his light and steer you on a course filled with joy. Accept his guidance, and then pivot.

John 12:46
"I have come as a light to shine in this dark world,
so that all who put their trust in me
will no longer remain in the dark."

I Met the Doctor Today

To maintain our relationship with Christ it's imperative to visit with Him on a regular basis. This poem describes one such visit.

I made an appointment with "the doctor" today,
I needed to hear what He had to say.
It's been so long, I was a little resistant,
"Come immediately" He was very insistent.

He checked my heart and offered a donor,
Jesus said yes—I am no longer a loner.
He checked my posture then aligned my walk,
After that, we had a great talk.

I listened closely, with joy I was filled,
The heat from the devil was surely chilled.
He provided some stories and sent some friends,
Who listened and supported right to the end.

He prescribed my therapy, including a cure,
He wrote on my heart with love so pure.
Pivotal choices were mine to make,
Positive changes were offered to take.

I made an appointment with the doctor today,
His love was felt, in my heart He'll stay.
Buoyed by his spirit, I know I'm ok,
I'm glad I met with "the doctor" today.

Have you met with Him? If not make an appointment today!

Matthew 11: 28-30
"Come to me, all of you who are weary & carry heavy burdens,
and I will give you rest. Take my yoke upon you. Let me teach you,
because I am humble and gentle at heart,
and you will find rest for your souls."

Full? or Fulfilled?

Is your life a rat race controlled by a calendar too small to handle all the commitments? Does it seem as if you are on a treadmill stuck on high? Are you saturated with stress, watered down with worry, or attacked by anxiety? If so— consider your life full.

Well God has a deal for you! His ageless product has helped millions find peace in a hectic world by giving them a sense of security and a home. It has lifted burdens that seemed too heavy to budge, and triggered miracles worldwide. It's called "surrender" and it's already wired into your being. All you have to do is activate it. When you surrender your life to Christ, He turns the fullness of life into a life that is fulfilled. Your calendar may be just as packed as before, but the events on it have a purpose. They are awash with the adventure of new learning, jam packed with the joy of love, and bountifully blessed by a community of friends.

So how does it work? Simply admit you are a sinner, ask Christ to join you, move over to the passenger seat, and ask Him to enter your life. By surrendering to Him, your focus switches from the mortal to the immortal. You move from selfish to selfless, from self-serving to servant hood. A partnership is formed and you will never be alone again. These dramatic switches trigger lifestyle changes that bring the peace and joy only God can provide.

By surrendering to God you are surrounding your life with his love. Only then can he fill your life in a way that makes it fulfilling.

John 10:9-10
"Yes, I am the gate. Those who come in through me will be saved. They will come and go freely and will find good pastures. The thief's purpose is to steal and kill and destroy. My purpose is to give them a rich and satisfying life."

Who Is Your Interior Decorator?

Good interior decorators are expert with color schemes, fashion trends and spatial symmetry. They are capable of making a house pleasing to the eye while projecting a personal statement to visitors. What decorators can't do is make a house a home. So what makes your house a home? Take a little stroll through it to look for evidence that goes beyond the visual and into the personal. I pray you may find some of the following items.

a. Evidence of **whose** you are. A cross or other Christian symbols. Not only do these serve as reminders to yourself, they also send a message that God is present in your home.
b. Evidence of **who** you are. Mementos or personal items depicting events in your life that have helped form your identity. Ask yourself "Do these reflect the real me? Is this the image I wish to project to society?"
c. Evidence of **love**. Search for memories of happy times and visuals of the people you love.

The ultimate interior decorator is the Holy Spirit. His guidance helps you make the right decisions. His assurance convinces you to be the person God intended. His constant vigilance supports a love so deep that you come to know nothing can separate you from God. His tender love washes over you with the knowledge that you are precious in God's eyes. This interior decorator is expert in living schemes, fashioning joyful lives, and bringing people in alignment to complement the symmetry of God's plan.

Interior decorators can make a house more pleasing to the eye, but God can make it a home. Let him decorate your personal interior because "home is where the Lord is."

Joshua 24:15
"But as for me and my family, we will serve the LORD."

Enjoy the Breeze

Have you ever spent a night in a non-air conditioned dorm room when the daytime high topped ninety degrees? The whole building radiates heat and creates a stuffy, uncomfortable environment. The air is stagnant. Sweat sits on your skin. It is a clammy unclean feeling. I am in such a place. Fortunately there is hope on the horizon because evening has arrived and I have found a fan. It is humming in a window delivering fresh cool air. This fan has changed my outlook on the prospect of sleeping.

Life can get stagnant and stuffy like this dorm room. The daily routines of living sometimes lead to laziness in our relationship with God and cause it to stagnate. This continues until you rediscover the Holy Spirit's power to rejuvenate. Like that fan in the window He blows comfort into your soul, which changes your outlook. The Spirit helps refocus your thoughts on Jesus and opens your heart to the joy he offers.

The fan creates a breeze, which speeds evaporation to cool you down. Likewise, as you pray, troubles begin to evaporate. Life becomes more comfortable and you rediscover joy in places you missed just days before. The heat of stress dissipates, relationships repair themselves, and the word "thanks" returns to your vocabulary. As prayer time increases, you seek out His wisdom more and more. Life is cool once again.

The hot, stuffy, unclean days are sure to return. The good news is this: The fan is in the room waiting to be turned on. The Holy Spirit is always willing to breathe the fresh air of Christ's love into our lives. Enjoy the breeze!

Romans 8:6
"So letting your sinful nature control your mind leads to death. But letting the Spirit control your mind leads to life and peace."

Breaking Through

"Trust in me" join a small group!
Just the thought throws me for a loop.

Go find a friend or two or three,
And get together, there I'll be.
It's hard at first and oh so scary,
But God will help so please don't tarry.

My past says don't try it, it's not for you,
My heart say's lets buy it, and get a clue.
My mind says I can't, my gut says I can.
Oh Lord give me courage to be real, as I am.

What will they think? Who will they see? …
You're right Lord …a lovely sinner valued by thee!

My walls are strong and hold me tight,
Is this who I am in your loving sight?
Is it safe? Can I let go?
Help me God, I want to grow!

I've tried it out and wish to shout,
Without a doubt my group has clout.

Accounting, love and sensibility,
These have created much stability.
We laugh, we cry, our spirits soar,
We trust, we love, our one true Lord.

I thank you God for being true
My walls are weak, I'm breaking through.
I'm happier, healthier, closer to being,
The precious one you've always seen.

My group is a stronghold, with them I will stand,
On solid foundations, your spirit at hand.
You said, "trust in me" and also in them:
With heart felt joy—I now say "Amen."

Tail Lights in the Twilight

Have you ever driven down a deserted road in a swirling snowstorm or soupy fog? These conditions make it extremely hard to stay on the road. Tightness develops in your arms as a knot of tension grows in the pit of your stomach. Every sensory bundle is on high alert as you focus on the task at hand. Time seems to crawl to a stop. You are all alone and wired for survival. Suddenly two pinpoints of red light appear at the edge of the murky horizon. Your grip on the wheel loosens as relief floods through your body. You are no longer alone. In fact you now have a companion whose light is leading the way. A sense of renewed safety is at hand.

God desires to be that set of lights for your life. As the swirl of worldly activities fog up your life, you need a companion to guide your way. Without Him you run the risk of leaving the road and crashing into the ditch Satan has prepared. When you do ask God into your life, He often sets Himself just ahead of you to light the path of righteousness. If you trust His guidance, a peace floods your body and allows for a relaxed grip on the steering wheel of life. He cuts through the fog of confusing decisions and calms the storms that appear out of nowhere, clearing the path for a safer trip.

Don't wait for bad weather to complicate your trip through life. Ask God to lead the way, and then follow His tail lights to the end of the road. It's your call: Try to do it alone, or ask for guidance. If you choose the latter, an eternal gift awaits you.

Luke 8:16
"No one lights a lamp and then covers it with a bowl or hides it under a bed. A lamp is placed on a stand, where its light can be seen by all who enter the house."

Individually Made

Several years ago there was an ad for taco fixings that had the catch phrase "What do you like more— Making them or eating them?" I had a hard time answering this question because tacos are fun to make but also delicious to eat. No two tacos are the same. Meat, onions, cheese, tomatoes and lettuce are added to a crispy shell in varying amounts then topped with some spicy sauce. The trick is to pack in as many fixings as possible without breaking the shell. My mouth waters as the taco creation takes form, begging to fulfill its ultimate purpose of nourishing my body. That is exactly what happens to every taco I have made. I guess that answers the original question: Eating tacos is more fun than making them.

I wonder how God would answer a similar question? "What do you like more— Creating people or seeing them fulfill their design?" I imagine Him getting great joy out of designing individuals. "I'll add a pinch of service, a dash of teaching, and a ounce of discernment. Then I'll top it off with a quick mind, some athletic ability and good health." No two designs are ever alike. Once packed within our human shell, He must stand back and beam with pride as each of us is born. Yet this pales in comparison to the joy God feels when His creations attain their ultimate purpose by using the gifts he bestowed on them. Each of us was created with a special blend of spiritual and physical gifts, but we all have one gift in common— A free will. This free will determines whether we become something good to look at, or something truly good.

James 2:17
" Faith by itself isn't enough.
Unless it produces good deeds,
it is dead and useless."

Disorder in the Court

How many times have you been reading a courtroom drama where the judge bangs his gavel and screams, "You are out of order, control yourself or you will be held in contempt." This always stops the behavior cold. Quite often this scene is a result of a calculated risk by a lawyer trying to gain an advantage for his client. Unfortunately we play this same game with our spiritual life. We bend a few rules, justify some shady behaviors and push the earthly envelope to gain a perceived advantage in our life. Then a friend confronts us, or we hear an inspired sermon and our conscience screams, "You are out of order, control yourself or you will be held in contempt." The behaviors stop cold, but the cycle begins anew because you are working for the wrong client – yourself.

There is a better way to live in the courtroom of our savior. Admit up front your life is out of order. Instead of fighting the judge, develop a friendship with Him. Move your life out of the courtroom and into your living room. By doing this, the focus swings away from the legalism of rules to the communion of love. You see, life is not about competency— it's about intimacy. Don't look to Him for a fix; ask Him to be in the mix of your imperfection. Let Him in to love you as you are. Only then can the sentences of guilt, shame, and isolation be granted a pardon. By getting to know the judge at a personal level you stop being adversaries and become one of His beneficiaries. Don't take this wrong, God is still the judge and you must try to play by His rules, but with Him by your side the inherent disorder in your life is reordered by his love and grace. Go ahead and testify for Him, then accept His verdict: An eternity of peace in His presence.

2 Timothy 4:7-8
"I have fought the good fight, I have finished the race, and I have remained faithful. And now the prize awaits me—the crown of righteousness, which the Lord, the righteous Judge, will give me on the day of his return. And the prize is not just for me but for all who eagerly look forward to his appearing."

Good Cooking

There are many ways to cook food. You can microwave it, fry it, bake it, barbecue it, or place it in a crock-pot. Each method has its own characteristics, but hopefully they all result in a tasty meal. Microwaves interact with the water in food resulting in a quick heat up. Frying immerses the food in a super heated bath. Barbecuing relies on direct flame. Baking and crock-pots use a lower heat source for slower cooking. Each process involves heat that chemically changes the ingredients. At the same time, microorganisms are destroyed preventing problems within our body.

A walk of faith is a similar process. Some people are placed in a microwave or frying pan situation and come out of it on fire for the Lord. Paul is an example of this type of Christian. On the way to Damascus he had a mighty encounter with God and quickly became a changed man. Others are baked like Jonah who was stewed in the stomach of a whale. Shadrach, Meshach, and Abednego confirmed their faith in God by resting in a fiery barbecue pit. Many biblical legends were slow cooked by God's heat over a long period of time. Abraham waited on God's promises. Moses repeatedly went to God for council. Joseph never gave up. Esther patiently waited on the lord. All were prepared by God's grace and changed into people of strong faith and conviction. They fed thousands of people and destroyed untold numbers of satanic advances.

We are more like these legends of the Old Testament than we think. If we let ourselves be infiltrated by the Holy Spirit, His fire will warm our hearts and cook us to perfection. This cooking results in a change for the better. So whether life throws you into fiery turmoil or slowly tries to tear you down — let God into your heart. Great stories might not be written about your accomplishments, but you can feed many people with the ingredients God placed within you.

Philippians 1:4-6
" I am certain that God, who began the good work within you,
will continue his work until it is finally finished
on the day when Christ Jesus returns."

A Firm Foundation

In many ways concrete is the foundation of our society. We drive on it, walk on it, and sometimes even sit on it. Buildings rest on concrete foundations, bridges are supported by it, and airplanes land on it. Concrete's versatility, strength and longevity combine to make it invaluable. Its liquid state can be shaped, yet hardens quickly. The cement that holds it together is a white powdery substance made by heating a mixture of limestone and clay. When mixed with water, sand and gravel, cement gains the characteristic of concrete. If this substance is poured around a web of rebar it becomes nearly indestructible.

Jesus is the cement of our faith. When faith is mixed with the blood of his crucifixion, the Holy Spirit, and the fellowship of believers, then poured into our spirit, it cements our faith. Jesus himself speaks of the strength of this faith in John 14:*12 "Very truly I tell you, whoever believes in me will do the works I have been doing, and they will do even greater things than these, because I am going to the Father."* Even greater works than Jesus? Wow! This is possible because we have that cement in our hearts, the Holy Spirit directing us, and our fellow believers supporting us.

God provides the ingredients for this concrete: He allowed His Son to come to Earth; He left His Holy Spirit to infiltrate all mankind; and He created the church so believers can gather together. But each of us must take one crucial action in order to make this spiritual concrete form in us. We must be the vessel that allows the mixing to occur. Ask Jesus to enter your life and cement a friendship with you. You can then build a joy-filled life on a solid foundation. Guaranteed for eternity.

Ephesians 2:20
"Together, we are his house, built on the foundation of the apostles and the prophets. And the cornerstone is Christ Jesus himself."

Putting Out Fires

Have you ever noticed how many fire hydrants there are scattered around the city? Virtually every home and business is within a few hundred feet of a hydrant. Each hydrant is ready to pour out tons of water at a moments notice. They can do so because water has been lifted up to a water tower. The pressure created by this reservoir fills the pipes leading to all hydrants so they are ready on demand. Should a fire threaten your home, the firemen need only attach a hose and open the valve to create a flood of water eager to squash the flaming inferno.

Like a fire hydrant, Jesus is ready to squash the fires of sin. He is always at-hand, never more than a moment away. If called upon he floods the situation with grace and forgiveness. He is able to accomplish this because he was lifted up to His father in Heaven where he now sits triumphant over evil. All you need to do is attach your heart to his loving kindness and the floodgates of heaven will burst forth to wash you clean.

Water and Jesus have a lot in common. Water is essential for life. So is He. Water is the most powerful cleanser on Earth; Jesus is the most powerful cleanser in the universe. Water exists in three phases, so does God. Water is purified each time it evaporates, so are we when we ask Jesus for forgiveness, Water is the main ingredient of blood, and Jesus' blood is the main ingredient in salvation.

Water is as essential to life on Earth as Jesus is to eternal life. He knows it, and I pray that you know it too. Drink in His water and live in the cleansing stream of his love forever.

John 4:14
"But those who drink the water I give will never be thirsty again.
It becomes a fresh, bubbling spring within them,
giving them eternal life."

Accept That You Have Been Accepted.

Lawyers spend their lives learning the law. Pharisees spent their lives interpreting the law. But does knowledge of the law always equate to keeping it? Jesus helped us realize that nobody can keep all the laws. He never dismissed the law as unnecessary; he focused on its unattainable nature. A life of legalism takes our focus off the "reasons we live" and places it squarely on "how we should live." Legalism creates guilt when we fall short, and self-righteousness when we don't. This legalistic attitude blinded the religious leaders of Christ's time to His teachings simply because the "laws" were being challenged. As a result they forfeited a chance at redemption, even as they orchestrated our redemption by crucifying Christ.

Jesus shattered the old laws by shifting their outward nature to our inner nature. Instead of living so God will accept you— live *because* God accepts you. He desires our wants not our deeds. I want to be saved. I want to know Jesus. I want to live a Christ centered life. I want to be the best I can be. These wants don't require rules they require relationships. Mark: 10 tells the story of a rich young man who followed all the rules but was unable to put God above all else. He rejected the comfort of Christ for the comfort of wealth. Yes, he followed the rules, but in the end was ruled by the wrong leader.

When you rearrange your life view from "I want to please you God" to "Please God I want you", the legalism of life takes a back seat to the new law of love.

John 13:34
"So now I am giving you a new commandment:
Love each other. Just as I have loved you,
you should love each other."

Voice Lessons

Many people have the gift of a beautiful voice— some for singing, some for speaking and others for dramatic inflections. To improve this gift they take voice lessons. The teacher's job is to fix minor imperfections, build up strength, and fine-tune tonal qualities. The student's job is to follow the advice of the teacher and practice. The result is a voice that communicates in a pleasing way. We definitely know when we hear such a voice.

What about God's voice? Too often we focus so much on our voice that we forget to train our ears to hear God's. Set apart some time to train with the Master by listening for his voice. At first you may have trouble pushing out the worldly noise making his voice hard to find. But believe this—you do have the ability to hear him speak. You may have to fine-tune your inner ear, but practice will help clear the airwaves. Once you start communicating with God you are automatically given a lifetime membership to his school of listening. The school offers personal lessons and is always open. He wants to teach us and guarantees results. Minor imperfections in your life will be fixed, spiritual strength will be increased, and you will be open to receiving His love.

If you desire to improve your voice, be sure to practice. If you desire to improve your life, ask God to help you listen for His voice. After a while His lessons will bring you to the point where you can say " I definitely know God's voice when I hear it." Listen up and learn — His voice lessens the worry and pain in life, and brings out the joy.

Isaiah 6:8
"Then I heard the Lord asking,
"Whom should I send as a messenger to this people?
Who will go for us?" I said, "Here I am. Send me."

Lord, You Were There

I went to church on Sunday morn
Your spirit was there and a bond was formed.
The song, the message, your story told
It all sank in; I was far from cold.

I bowed once more for final prayer
I knew dear Lord that you were there.

I went to work and acted bold
Prayed for bickering to be put on hold.
Invited two others to form a group
We met at lunch over coffee and soup.
We read the word and ended in prayer
I knew, dear Lord that you were there.

I went to the hospital to visit a friend
She was glad to see me and on the mend.
We chatted about life then started to pray
The doctor arrived ending my stay.
I left with assurance she was in good care
I knew, dear Lord that you were there.

I sat with my family at supper one night
We prayed, we talked, the food was right.
The bonds we felt were deep and true
We enjoyed each other through and through.
I realized how much my family cares
I knew, dear Lord that you were there.

Reflect on times you have been with others and asked Jesus to join
you. I bet you will be able to tell that He was there.

Matthew 18: 19-20
"For where two or three gather together as my followers,
I am there among them."

The Doctor is "In"

Why do we often resist going to the doctor until we have suffered more than we need to? For me it's because I have not taken care of my body and am a little fearful of what the doctor will tell me. It's easier to push things to the back of your mind and hope they will go away. The problem is, they won't go away and, yes, habits and lifestyles may have to change before we can get healthy.

We often deal with faith issues in the same manner. As we start feeling some distance from God, our comfort level diminishes and joy starts seeping out of our lives. Yet we resist asking our doctor for help. Whether it is a sense of unworthiness or pressures from society that keep us from making an appointment with Jesus, the results are the same. There is an increase in sin and a decrease in joy. Spiritual health depends on daily checkups with Jesus and periodic inventories of our behaviors. It doesn't stop there however. We need to listen to what the doctor says and stay faithful to the treatment He prescribes.

Medical doctors heal physical ailments; Jesus heals both spiritual and physical. Medical doctors prescribe treatments that often work. Jesus' treatments always work. Medical doctors maintain schedules and are accessible at certain times. Jesus' schedule simply reads: **"The doctor is in"**. He set up his practice on a cross 2000 years ago and began seeing patients on Easter morning. Make an appointment with the doctor today.

John 3:16-17
"For God loved the world so much that he gave his one and only Son, so that everyone who believes in him will not perish but have eternal life. God sent his Son into the world not to judge the world, but to save the world through him."

Use Your God Sense

Why is it so hard to believe people who say they hear God speaking to them? We live in a world of reception. TV and radio waves fill our atmosphere waiting to be received by antenna and turned into sounds. Light waves bathe our earth and are continually received by our sense of sight. Objects all around us are felt by nerve receptors; odors are smelled, food is tasted. Our senses are detecting things all the time. But these sense organs can't process the information gained. They send it to our brain for interpretation.

Our brain is the true source of all we perceive. It is here that light is seen and sound is heard. So why is it such a stretch for us to accept the possibility that God's voice can be received and interpreted? If he gave us senses to experience the physical world he surely must have given us senses to experience the spiritual world. All we have to do is quiet the worldly information flooding our brain and focus on receiving His voice. It may come as a feeling, or as a creative thought. It may take the form of a dream or of an actual voice. How about intuition, premonition, or inspiration? Some people talk about our inner voice and our conscience. All of these things are interpretations created within our minds. Where is their input source? — Probably your God sense.

Create some quiet time. Close down the bombardment of worldly input and tune your inner antenna to the voice of God. Your God sense will receive His voice in its own special way. God wants a personal relationship with you. A great way to build that relationship is with a friendly chat. May the voice you hear move from your mind, to your heart, and fill it with peace.

2 Corinthians 12:6
"I don't want anyone to give me credit beyond what they can see in my life or hear in my message."

Shell Games

Remember the old magic trick that involves 3 cups and a ball? The magician puts a ball under a cup, quickly moves the cups around and asks you to find the ball. It seems so easy, but you can't succeed unless the magician wants you to. This is how Satan works in our lives. He makes things seem easier than they are and tries to convince you to choose the wrong path. He even tried it on Jesus by offering great gifts for the simple act of bowing down to him. Satan tried to turn Jesus. Jesus didn't fall for it. He stayed true to his Father and chose the harder but right path. As a result we gained salvation.

Shell games can be cleverly packaged and often promise personal gain. Get rich schemes, gambling, promiscuity, the list goes on. Like the shell game itself however, they are based on deception. Satan (a master magician) is controlling the cups. What shell games have you been tempted to enter? Whatever they are, you can be sure of two things. First, they aren't as enticing as they appear. Each one contains hidden pitfalls guaranteed to muddle your life and pull you away from God (AKA sin). Second, no matter when you ask God for help, whether before getting sucked into the game, or after getting involved, God <u>will</u> be able to expose the lie. He makes the cups transparent so you can see what is really going on. He will also help you restore any losses and get started anew. All you have to do is admit your mistake and ask for forgiveness.

If you think the shell game is a thing of the past think again. The story of Christ's temptation in Luke 4 ended with, *" When the devil had finished all his tempting, he left him until an opportune time."* Beware of shell games—they do exist.

Luke 4: 1,13
"Jesus replied, "The Scriptures say, You must worship the LORD your God and serve only him."

Voice Recognition

Computers have the capability of recognizing voices. Before it can be activated by a voice, however, it must first be taught to recognize it. How is your voice recognition software working? Since the beginning of time God has communicated with us using prophets, miracles and an inner voice, yet many believe direct communication with God has ceased.

Don't buy into this! His communication system is state-of-the-art and available to anyone who wants to access it. So how do we tap into it? First, we must adjust our receiver. The atmosphere is full of electromagnetic energy carrying messages via television and radio waves. Unless we tune into these, they just bounce around and are never received. To understand electromagnetic waves, you need to study the physics behind them. To understand God, you must study His word. The Bible will help you tune your spiritual receiver.

Second, we need to recognize God when He does talk. This requires a relationship with Him, like the one describing the good shepherd in John 10. We are the sheep in this story. If we know our Master and follow His call, we will be safe and secure. The Good Shepherd can't help the sheep that don't know Him.

Third, we need faith. Hebrews 11 recounts great stories of many heroes in the Old Testament who acted on their faith. Did they hear the voice of God? Absolutely— and they responded in faith. Like them, we must respond when God calls.

As a myriad of voices bombard us in today's hectic world we need a good voice-activated communication system that allows us to input both praise and fears. That system exists. It comes with free installation and lifetime warranty. Open your heart to God and let His voice activate your life.

John 10:27
"My sheep listen to my voice; I know them, and they follow me."

Master Carpenter

I recently spent a delightful Saturday with four other men building a deck. A local retreat center had crumbling stairways for two entrances. We had volunteered to help make these safer by connecting them with a deck and common staircase. It felt good using my limited carpentry skills to help this project get completed. We couldn't have done it however, without the help of a master carpenter. Jim showed up with all the necessary tools, plus the skills to direct our group of willing guys. Prior to our arrival, Jim had arranged for the foundations to be built. Now it was time to start building. He designed, measured, cut, and instructed us in installation as we pieced the deck together. The air tools, drills, and saws were instrumental in allowing the project to come together in one day. We left that evening confident in a job well done.

Jim was the essential piece of our crew. Without him and his tools the rest of us could not have completed this project. Jesus is the essential piece, the master carpenter, of the project called life. He laid the foundation before we were born by sacrificing himself on the cross. He possesses all the tools, knows how a joyful life is designed, and is willing to share all of this with us. Our role is to volunteer to be on His crew. We need to recognize this and center our life on top of it. The tools of life were given in unique combinations. God shares his design ideas with us via the Bible. It's all there waiting to be discovered. He knows how to use each person's skills to build a solid deck from which to enter, enjoy, and exit life.

Whatever project life requires we are free to volunteer Jesus as our master carpenter. He is willing and available to direct us. Without him we can fumble through life using our God given talents. With him we can joyfully succeed in this life and beyond. Start building a new life with our master carpenter. The views from the decks he helps you build are both beautiful and everlasting.

Ephesians 2:20
"Together, we are his house… And the cornerstone is Christ Jesus."

His Presence – Our Present

Christmas morning: families gathering, gifts unwrapped, joyful smiles, thanks shared. Sound familiar? Christmas day truly is special. A lot of preparation goes into making it a day to remember. Yet invariably these memories fade and the world rises up to pull us back into the hustle of life.

God also put a lot of preparation into making that first Christmas a day to remember. He created us with a free will then laid the groundwork for helping us make wise decisions. Throughout the Old Testament, God gave the gifts of prophets and protection, covenants and commandments, leaders and lessons. Humans opened these presents and accepted His gifts with thankful hearts. Yet each time memories faded and the world rose up to pull them away from God.

Thankfully God never gave up on us. Over time He patiently worked to convince us of His love. But we really didn't get it— our memories always faded. Then 2000 years ago God gave us the ultimate present— His presence on Earth. Many of us have unwrapped this gift, said thanks for it, and shared it with others. But do we use it often enough? This is a present to be used daily in all we do. It is a present with many other presents wrapped inside: Peace that passes all understanding, the promise of help anytime anywhere, companionship when we are lost or lonely, a friend for life, and salvation from sin and spiritual death.

Hopefully Christmas memories can bring a smile to your face and joy to your heart. I pray that God's presence will be the greatest present you ever receive.

Ephesians 3:12
"Because of Christ and our faith in him, we can now come boldly and confidently into God's presence."

The Word
John 1

" In the beginning the Word already existed. He was with God, and he was God. He was in the beginning with God. He created everything there is. " On Christmas morning the Word became flesh as a tiny baby in a manger. God's ultimate gift was sent to remind us of his unending love.

"Life itself was in him, and this life gives light to everyone." Brilliant starlight shone forth that night in Bethlehem heralding new life for mankind, a light seen through the whole world announcing the new covenant. This covenant involves love and grace, is available to all that believe, and bears a promise of everlasting life.

"The light shines through the darkness, and the darkness can never extinguish it." The shepherds and wise men responded to this light and their lives were changed forever. To this day people can draw upon the strength of His light to help them through dark times. Never has the light failed to penetrate the darkness in order to kindle a fire of peace, and light our path. It never will be defeated— guaranteed!

Pause for a moment and reflect on examples in your life when you trusted in Jesus. Allow His peace to flow through you. Be a light to those around you. Bow down and give him thanks for coming into this world on Christmas morning to save you. May His word be your word. May your light shine forth for others to see so they too will believe.

John 1:1-5 & 14
"The Word gave life to everything that was created,
and his life brought light to everyone."

V-I-C-T-O-R-Y

Fall Friday nights mean high school football. The weather is often cool, but emotions are hot as the hometown team enters the stadium amid music and cheers. Cheerleaders get people riled up with V-I-C-T-O-R-Y – victory—victory that's our cry!" Pride is obvious and expectations high. The game is about to begin.

Wouldn't it be great if Sunday mornings were also like this? Imagine Christians joyfully entering their place of worship with expectations of a great victory. Cheering for Christ through praise and worship. The band leads us in song and the minister delivers an inspirational pep talk. The game is about to begin.

A fan's role in football is confined to cheering. They have little direct impact on the outcome. The same is true for people who attend Sunday worship and check their Christianity at the door on the way out. They become fans in the stands.

Have you fully joined Christ's team? Or are you cheering from the sidelines? Show your pride by talking up your faith. Get into the game by sharing your talents and spreading God's love. Push yourself to connect with God daily through scripture and prayer. Invite others to join you. Do it in the name of our hometown team "The Christians." Boldly step forward and score touchdowns for Christ.

Football is fun to watch, and good for the community, but its victories are just that: a win, something to talk about and take pride in. Christianity is much more. Victory in Christ changes your life for eternity. Join us in the stands during worship and then march out onto the field and do battle the rest of the week.

Oh, by the way, in football the best team doesn't always win. On Christ's team victory is guaranteed. Get with THE winner and experience His ultimate victory.

Romans 8:38
"I am convinced that nothing can ever
separate us from God's love."

DEFENSE! DEFENSE!

It is third and goal late in a close football game as your team digs in. The crowd is on its feet roaring, "defense". The game is on the line. Many say, "good offense wins games, but good defense wins championships." Our spiritual game is also on the line. If we build a strong defense against Satan, we will win the crown at the end of our season. Consider how the following ingredients help fortify our spiritual defense.

Teamwork: If we try to resist temptation on our own we will fail. Those who ask God for help, and back this up with support from a small group have accountability on their side. This beefs up resistance to Satan and plugs the holes caused by sin before they get too large.

Knowledge: By reading God's word we equip ourselves with identification tools that help avoid temptation. We also gain wisdom in the areas of grace and forgiveness. These are valuable recovery tools when we give up yardage and start distancing ourselves from God.

Skill: God given talents and practice combine to form this crucial ingredient. Each of us has been given unique and valuable gifts but unless we identify and practice them, they lie dormant. A rusty talent is slow to react and often fails to perform properly when called on to stop the opponent.

Team Pride: Putting on the armor of God and standing tall in your beliefs requires action. There should be no doubt in your mind as to whose team you are on. With pride on your side you create boldness, helping you tackle whatever life throws at you.

By building a strong defense we create more time for our offense to go onto the field and advance the kingdom of God. The game of life does have a final buzzer and there are both winners and losers. I pray that your defense is solid enough to push Satan back into his end zone so you can enjoy the safety of God's love.

Ephesians 6:11
"Put on all of God's armor so that you will be able to stand firm against all strategies of the devil."

The Faith–Bottomed Boat

I recently went to a boat show and was amazed at the variety of watercraft. I saw every imaginable type and size of boat. Some were built for speed; others for leisure, but the ones that attracted me most were the ones built for living on. Everything one desires for an extended safe and comfortable trip was built into these beauties. They had soft leather couches for lounging; a spacious room for gathering when night falls or weather gets inclement, cooking facilities for dining, even bedrooms, and bathrooms complete with showers. Each had huge engines ready to push you through the water and navigation tools to help you stay safe while on the trip. All of them had one thing in common— a durable hull that kept them afloat.

God provides us with a boat to help us navigate the waters of life. He calls her "Faith". She has all the amenities mentioned above— shelter from storms, navigation devices to help us stay on the right path, comfortable places to rest when we get weary, and a shower of grace to cleanse us when we sin. Powered by the Holy Spirit, "Faith" has an endless supply of fuel and plenty of power to move us along at a steady speed. "Faith" however has one important feature that all boats at the show lacked— no physical hull. A marvelous sight greets you as you look into her holds to see nothing but water. What keeps her afloat? It goes against all human comprehension, but that doesn't concern us. We know God built "Faith" and He is the master creator. So we continue our journey on the river of life, confident in His love, anticipating great joy at the end of the cruise.

Hebrews 11
"Faith is the confidence that what we hope for will actually happen; it gives us assurance about things we cannot see."

Changed Lives

I just returned from the high school graduation party of a close family friend. Up to ninth grade this shy young man was somewhat of a loner involved in a minimum of activities. Things changed dramatically during the next four years. By getting involved he discovered his gifts and utilized them to the fullest. Speech, drama, and music became the tools of maturity. He excelled in all, eventually becoming class president and giving the graduation speech to 500 classmates. He is now a confident person with a world of opportunities ahead of him.

I experienced the same type of transformation in my faith. At the age of thirty I decided to get involved in the ministry of our church. God has done a great work in me through this involvement. All aspects of my life have changed for the better as I discovered God given talents and used them to further His kingdom.

Neither my wife nor I started as confident individuals who believed we had talents to offer. Both of us now understand that we do. What is the commonality between us? We got involved in safe environments that allowed us to stretch. By serving we were in turn served. This opportunity is available to all who take the initiative to get involved. There is no safer place to do this than your church community. God guarantees that He will never put too many burdens on us and will always be there to support and guide us. So if you are looking for a positive change in your life, take a chance and get involved. You won't be alone and will not be the only beneficiary of this decision. Everyone you serve will also experience some change. The world will be just a little bit better as a result.

Matthew 11:29
"Take my yoke upon you. Let me teach you, because I am humble and gentle at heart, and you will find rest for your souls."

Heart Transplant

Thousands of people's lives are saved each year due to the gift of organ transplants. Sadly, the donor often died in order to make the gift available. This is definitely true for heart transplants. The good news is this. Medical science has advanced to become very successful in the field of heart transplantation. Each year, hundreds of lives are restored replacing despair with hope, and infirmary with health. The process begins when a donor with a healthy heart becomes brain dead. Matches are made and a recipient identified then prepped. This prep includes removing all but a critical bit of the damaged heart. The new heart is sewn in place and the crucial startup procedure begins. Recovery follows as the recipient starts the healing process. A new life begins with a changed heart. It is important to note here that only whole hearts can be transplanted.

There is another type of heart transplant that has been perfected. It's a spiritual heart transplant available to all people who desire a new and healthier life. Jesus offered to donate his heart by dying on a cross. In order to be a perfect match all you have to do is believe in His desire to heal you. Permission is as easy as asking to be healed. Prep involves admitting your sinful nature while surrendering your will to His. Surgery is pain free but recovery involves some work. Habits need changing. A tiny piece of your old heart remains signifying the original beauty of your unique creation while reminding us that we are still human.

With a new heart, life becomes wonderfully different. Jesus has filled you with love, pumping grace into your life, delivering a peace that only His heart can provide. If your life is short of breath, lacks stamina, and includes blurry vision; consider a heart transplant. This is why Jesus came to Earth. Through his death He offered new life.

When Jesus calls, accept His invitation, for he is the ultimate lifesaver. Please discuss the topic of organ donation with your family. It may end up saving a life.

Proverbs 23:26
"O my son, give me your heart"

Fireworks

I can't remember a year when I've missed a Fourth of July fireworks show. Thousands of people flock to the site flooding the streets in search of an open area with a good view. Families settle into scattered bundles on blankets to anxiously wait for darkness to fall and rockets to rise. Then it begins. Globes of light and percussive booms shatter the night sky in a symphony of color and sound. It's the type of show that rivets the audience through the brilliance of its light and unleashed power. Fireworks truly are a great way to celebrate Independence Day.

They also make a fitting symbol of our Christian faith. Christ burst onto the scene 2000 years ago lighting up lives with a message of hope and forgiveness. The power of light is clearly evident in the Fourth of July skies just as the power of love is evident in His grace. Jesus often made bold statements that sent waves of noise throughout the established church. (These "booms" were part of the foundation for establishing His new covenant). Law was replaced by love and showmanship was replaced with servant hood. He often preached to great crowds spread in family groups and their attention was riveted by the bursts of words that sent wonder and awe through their veins. He opened their hearts to a new way of life, which conquered darkness and shed light on the hope of salvation. For this we are eternally grateful.

In some respects Jesus was a walking, talking fireworks display who boldly proclaimed our independence from sin. Try adding the qualities of a fireworks show to your life. With God's help your light can shine to brighten the world around you.

Psalm 33:12
"What joy for the nation whose God is the LORD,
whose people he has chosen as his inheritance."

Extraordinary Ordinary People

We know them collectively as the 12 disciples. They were chosen by Jesus to spread the new gospel of love and grace. Why them? They certainly weren't educated world leaders or even men of high social standing. There were 5 fishermen, one tax collector and 6 men of unknown occupations. By earthly standards they were definitely ordinary. Jesus was making a statement right from the start of his ministry. He came to save all people. His ministry was not interested in social status or power. It was all about the status of the heart.

The disciples set everything aside to follow Jesus and approached their ministry with servant hearts. Peter, James, John, Andrew, and Philip turned in their nets to become fishers of men. Matthew left a corrupt life and became one of the first to accept God's grace. Bartholomew was a true fan who stood up for his beliefs. Thomas had trouble believing without physical proof, Jesus provided it and Thomas never doubted again. James and Thaddeus were not very outspoken, yet stayed faithful and dedicated to Jesus. Simon was a patriot willing to stand up and fight for righteousness. And Judas, unable to give up worldly desires, gave in to temptation. As individuals none stood out as world leaders, yet collectively they were able to get the world's attention to launch Christ's church.

Most of us are just like these twelve, pretty ordinary by worldly standards, but extraordinary in God's eyes. He gave each one of us talents and gifts to be used to further his kingdom. Together we can change the world. Trust in your capabilities, and join with others to spread the Gospel. Expect great results when you join His team of servants, because Jesus turns the ordinary into the extraordinary.

Romans 12:4-5
"Just as our bodies have many parts and each part has a special function, so it is with Christ's body. We are many parts of one body, and we all belong to each other."

Let Your Light Shine Forth

I have had the privilege of working with youth. Through them I have learned how to let my light shine forth. They have taught me much and helped me understand the personal nature of God's love. Each time I reached out to help them I was helped in return. That's God's way. When we step forward and shine our light, His love is received, then, passed on. No "thank you" is expected in return. Recently however I received a thank you letter that moved me deeply. From third grade through High School, Becca was an active member of our church's youth and a family friend. Her letter reads, "This past week I attended an in-service about helping kids be resilient. The research shows one or two significant adults make a big difference in the life of a child. This makes me think of you and how you were a very positive presence in my growing up years. As a Sunday school teacher, family friend, and caring mentor— you were there for me in many ways. So, I wanted to take a minute to let you know that you have made a difference in the life of a child— and I appreciate all the positive things you've added to my life."

I share this now not to bring attention to myself, instead it is a great reminder of the power of God's love and the impact of a thank you. Each of us has talents to share. Too often we hide them under a basket, but when we let them shine forth as God intended, lives are changed. What about that thank you? It too is a gift from God we don't share enough. Thank you notes are battery chargers that result in more powerful lights.

Reflect on who your significant role models are. Thank God for their presence in your life and consider recharging their batteries with a note. Don't stop there however. Let your light shine on the heart of a child so the Lord may fill it with Joy.

Matthew 5:14
"You are the light of the world—
like a city on a hilltop that cannot be hidden."

Teamwork

If you have ever gone on a canoe trip, you understand the value of teamwork. Each trip needs a guide and a map to show the way, but the group functions best when all people share the duties. At the close of each day, tents need to be pitched, wood gathered, supper cooked, and gear stowed for the night— all before the mosquitoes tell you its time for bed. If one or two people do the bulk of the work, tension mounts and joy diminishes. If, on the other hand, all group members assume a servant's heart and pitch in willingly, the group bonds together, making tasks less cumbersome. This bond becomes as important as the wilderness experience itself. The journey becomes a process not just a destination.

When we take responsibility to serve others, societal barriers dissolve, egos are held in check, and teamwork becomes the norm. A cord is created binding the group together while strengthening each individual. As Paul stated in Philippians 2:3-4, *"Do nothing out of selfish ambition or vain conceit. Rather, in humility value others above yourselves, not looking to your own interests but each of you to the interests of the others."*

The trick is to take this team attitude and apply it to all aspects of our lives. If we approach life like those on the canoe trip mentioned above, joy will follow us wherever we travel. God has a destination in mind for each one of us. He provides the guide (Holy Spirit) and the map (Bible). Jesus set the example and desires for us to join His team by serving others. If you say, "yes" to this journey it will be filled with loving moments plus joyful experiences. You will be truly amazed at how well His team works.

Philippians: 2:5
"You must have the same attitude that Christ Jesus had."

The Cure

One of my favorite movies is <u>Medicine Man</u>. The story takes place deep in the rainforest and focuses on a reclusive scientist who is sure he has discovered the cure for cancer. Unfortunately he is unable to reproduce the working serum. He places his trust in the belief the chemical needed is found in the epiphytes, a flower that grows high in the forest canopy and uses the trees for support. Near the end of the movie it is revealed the answer lies not in the epiphytes but in the ants that use this flower as a home. Tragically a fire destroys the entire area before he can collect any ants. The discovery came too late to help him. The movie ends with him wandering deeper into the jungle to start over.

Too many people make this same mistake with faith. By putting their faith in worldly relationships they miss the opportunity to discover the cure for everlasting peace. His name is Jesus Christ. A relationship with Him will cure you for eternal life. If you know of someone who is searching for truth in the wrong places, help them discover God's truth. Don't wait until it's too late. No true friend would allow someone to lose everything in the fires of hell and wander lost in an existence devoid of God's love.

Luke 12:21
"Yes, a person is a fool to store up earthly wealth
but not have a rich relationship with God."

Beginnings and Endings

As New Years Day approaches the world focuses on what lies ahead and what is behind. We analyze the good and bad from the past year in hopes of improving next year. This often leads to resolutions made, and an excitement of better things to come. I love this time of year.

As a teacher, I get to begin and end three times each year. We change students on a trimester basis. As a trimester comes to an end we hustle to finalize grades, the kids make sure they have done everything they can to earn the best grade possible and everyone prepares for the final test. Then suddenly everything changes: new classes, new topics, and a fresh start for all.

God also loves beginnings and endings. Imagine his joy as He created this world as described in Genesis 1:31, *"God saw all that he had made, and it was very good."* Feel his pride on Christmas morning as Jesus lay in Mary's arms. Imagine his love as Christ died on the cross to rise again in three days. God created us to rule this Earth. He sent Jesus to rule our hearts. He allowed Christ to die in order to rule our salvation.

Any day can be New Year's Day for us. Grade yourself if you wish, then give praise for your accomplishments, ask for forgiveness, and throw away the report card. The past is forgiven and forgotten, a new year dawns and we are given a new beginning. He is the Alpha and Omega, the beginning, and the end. What began on Christmas day was fulfilled on Easter morning, salvation for all who accept eternal grace through Jesus Christ. Happy New Year!

Isaiah 41:4
"Who has done such mighty deeds,
summoning each new generation from the beginning of time?
It is I, the LORD, the First and the Last. I alone am he."

The Bet

You have seen it many times in the movies. A high stakes poker game in which someone has placed more on the table than he can afford. This person tries to control his emotions to portray a calm, confident front. We call it a poker face. Yet inside, he is a bundle of nerves filled with an uncertain edge of doubt. As each card is viewed and decisions made, tensions mount leading to a certain end. One will win the others lose. No ties or second chances, he has entrusted his future to the turn of the cards.

Each of us must play out this scene in a slightly different manner. The stakes go beyond our personal possessions to our priceless protection. The bet is this: "Does God really exist?" Many try to bluff their way through the answer. On the outside they do all the right things to make it look like they know the answer. On the inside they are filled with doubt but afraid to show it in fear of losing a reputation. Others flatly say "no" and challenge us to prove them wrong. A third group answers "yes" and backs this up with a calm confidence. They exude a peace, which guides them through the whole ordeal with a smile on their face and hope in their heart. When asked how they maintain this composure they answer: " It's simple — If God doesn't exist, belief or non belief doesn't matter. If God does exist and you don't believe — you lose! If God exists and you do believe — you win." I chose to believe, and have been blessed by that decision ever since. How about you? Please don't entrust your eternal life to the chance of earthly circumstances. Bet on God and become a winner for all eternity.

John 6:35
"Jesus replied, "I am the bread of life.
Whoever comes to me will never be hungry again.
Whoever believes in me will never be thirsty."

Home for the Holidays

A big part of any holiday is going home to reconnect with loved ones. Just being in each other's presence brings joy to our hearts. This is especially true at Christmas, where the added dimension of giving, allows for a physical expression of love.

Did you ever stop to think about where Jesus was on that first Christmas morning? He wasn't at home. He had left the comforts of His home to visit ours. Wow! What a gift! In fact, all the characters in the Christmas story were away from home that night. The shepherds were working; Mary and Joseph were traveling; and the wise men were searching. These people were chosen to proclaim the Good News that the Christ child had arrived in our home. Their actions and reactions spoke volumes to generations to come. The shepherds were in awe at the sight of the new shepherd and then spread the news. Mary and Joseph tenderly cared for their child who needed parents to nurture his growth. The wise men brought gifts and marked him with the seals of royalty. God was presenting his gift to us in the form of Jesus.

On Christmas morning, Jesus left his home to offer us a new one. A place where we will reconnect with loved ones and experience the joy of *His* presence. God presented us with the ultimate gift: His one and only son. Have you accepted it?

May holidays find you surrounded by loved ones who know about the Christmas invitation to "come home for the holiday" that we call heaven.

John 1:12
"But to all who believed him and accepted him,
he gave the right to become children of God."

Go and Tell

A retelling of the Easter story found in Matthew 21 – 28.

Oh what a story about a King who is coming.
He is gentle and humble, yet will cause a great rumble.
On a donkey he rides through a sea of humanity.
They knew nothing about the impending calamity.

Go and tell— And so they did. Be like them, give God a strong bid.

Oh what a reception of palms and praise.
"Hosanna in the highest" their voices did raise.
Blessed is he, who comes from God.
Hosanna in the highest, on palms he did trod.

Go and tell— That Jesus saves. The King is here and here to stay.

Oh what a statement as he trashed the temple.
For all to see, as he set an example.
"My temple will be a house of prayer.
Not a den for thieves, or the devils lair."

Go and tell— Stop; then pray. Know Christ is with you all the way.

Oh what a faith as he dried up a fig.
It withered and shrunk to a miniature twig.
"You who have faith- just ask— it will be.
Accept this gift from my Father and me."

Go and tell— Expect great things.
Relay the truth His message brings.

Oh what a thinker as he turned traps into truths.
Stories he told to help us bear fruit.
Do we pay taxes to Caesar a king?
To whom do we bow? And what should we bring?
"Give to Caesar what is Caesar's, to God what is God's."
Materials will vanish while Heaven applauds.

Go and tell— Our God is greater.
The ruler of life—The Father creator.
Oh what a predicament as he accuses church leaders.

He spoke without fear and accosted those bleeders.
"You hypocrites, you makers and breakers of rules.
You judges of people are nothing but fools.
You who give gifts with dull empty hearts.
You will be judged and from Heaven depart!"

Go and tell— Don't put on airs.
Be whom you are, a person who cares.

Oh what a promise of the future he tells.
Claims of today and laws he dispels.
The temple will tumble, evil will dwell.
Be strong to the end, for all will be well.
Be ready at all times, like a thief in the night.
"I will return to take home those who know wrong from right."

Go and tell— With a servant's heart.
Dwell on his words & do your part.

Oh what a plot to end his life.
Throughout the land it would bring great strife.
Find a betrayer— determine a spot.
Make up some evidence to back up the plot.
Trump up the charges and charge up the crowds.
Get people to shout "Barrabas" real loud.

Go and tell— For reasons real.
Don't judge or accuse— be the real deal.

Oh what a dinner in a room up above.
Friends are together for a supper of love.
"As it is written you will lose your faith.
To help you regain it I give you my plate.
Take and eat for this is my flesh.
Do it with faith and be refreshed.
Take and drink for this is my blood.
Then into your heart my spirit will flood."

Go and tell— So all may remember.
Share with others a love so tender.

Oh what a Friday so dark and dreary.
Its pain so strong its hours so teary.
He is whipped, bloodied, taunted and cursed.
Yet accepts it all as he did from birth.
Lifted in pain on a cross so bare.
A horrifying sight for all who were there.
To save humanity, he sacrificed life.
Then returned home and give us new life.

Go and tell— of the pain he suffered.
So all may know new life is offered.

Oh what a miracle and oh what a sight.
For the tomb is empty and the endings just right.
Alleluia! Praise the Lord.
Alleluia! He is adored.
He has gone to his Father new life has been given.
We're rejoicing on Earth just as is Heaven.
Jesus Christ is risen today.
His love is great and here to stay.

Go and tell— Death is defeated.
With joy so great it must be repeated.

Spread the news! Beat your drum!
Today is Easter! Our Lord has come!

Oh what a story 2000 years old.
A story so wondrous it must be retold.
If not told by Christians, then by whom?
Remember this, "Christ is counting on you!"

Life Trails From the Past

Crossing paths with biblical characters

We have heard and read the stories of people in the Bible. What if we could listen to them tell their own stories and give us advice on topics relevant today? Following are testimonies as if written by biblical heroes. The people's stories are real; these dialogs are expansions of their reality.

.

May you find connections between their stories and your stories.

Psalm 107:1
" Give thanks to the LORD, for he is good!
His faithful love endures forever.

Trust Me

My name is Noah. At the beginning of time God made Heaven & Earth. The Earth was empty, and darkness was upon it. Then God said, "Let there be light"; and there was light. God saw that the light was good, and He separated the light from the darkness.

But soon things turned sour. Adam and Eve tried to become like God and humanity fell. Cain murdered his brother Abel starting a downward spiral in human behavior. The Earth became corrupt in God's sight and was filled with violence. My neighbors had become Godless, thinking only of themselves and the light dimmed. It was hard growing up in this environment, yet I stayed true to my God.

My nickname could have been No, but I stood with my God and the results changed history. "Build an ark," He said. I asked "Why me? There are better carpenters, I am not very good with animals, and I am old." I responded, "You have the gifts of faith, perseverance, and honor. These are traits I want to repopulate the Earth with, so build an ark." Then I asked, "What for?" God said, "Trust me". That is what I needed to hear. I did trust in my Lord and decided to embark on this mammoth project.

He was right. I was the man for the job. I finished the ark, rode out the storm, and survived with enough animals to repopulate the earth. God's trust in me and mine in Him rewrote the history of life on Earth. Not only was I blessed; I was given the glorious light of a rainbow signifying a new covenant between God and mankind.

God offers His light to all who believe in Him. That light shines today and darkness will never overcome it.

**Have you ever done something out of the ordinary
in order to spread God's light?**

Prepared for Success

I am Jonah, son of Armittai. My tale may sound fishy to you, but it really happened. I lived in a time when Assyria ruled the world. This great empire was known for its cruelty. No city lived up to this reputation more than its capital, Ninevah. When God commanded me to go there and warn this sinful city to repent, my stomach churned with hatred. They weren't worthy of anything but destruction. So what did I do? I ran. I wanted nothing to do with helping those heathens. But God had other plans and refused to let me off the hook. A great storm struck my escape ship forcing the sailors to throw me overboard in order to save their lives. I thought I was a dead man and knew in my heart I deserved to die. To my amazement a great fish swallowed me whole— and there I sat for three days contemplating my fate.

Locked there in the prison of the dead, I had lost all hope. It was then that I turned back to the Lord. I came to appreciate God's mercy and realized I was no more deserving of forgiveness than the Ninevites. Yet, He desired to save both. I was spat out of the fish and once again commanded to go to Nineveh. This time I did. With God at my side, I was able to convince this city to repent, resulting in its salvation from destruction.

I wish I could say I was immediately grateful, but I wasn't. My pride got in the way and I once again got angry with the Lord because he had spared the city. I sat on a hilltop and brooded. It took God several days to convince me to look outside of myself to feel compassion for the people of Nineveh. I thank him daily for His patient persistence and am in awe of the depth of His love for His people. God chose me for an important ministry. It wasn't until I accepted His will and followed His desires that I came to grips with both my weaknesses and gifts. I pray that you too will come to realize His will for you, and despite your weaknesses, understand that He has prepared you for success.

Is there someone in your life that you need to forgive?

Heavenly Hope

I am Moses; born to a Hebrew mother, raised as a prince of Egypt, matured in the wilderness as a shepherd, then chosen by God to lead His people to freedom. I enjoyed wealthy comfort, endured penniless hardship, survived stressful leadership, and found joy by experiencing God. I never backed away from trouble or looked for the easy way out. My dedication to God and his people was unfaltering (only once did I try to take credit away from him and paid dearly for this transgression.) My life was filled with changes, challenges, and charges. I thank God for each chapter because I know He never left my side and always was in control.

I was born at a time of unrest for the Egyptian Hebrews. We were an enslaved people who for some reason threatened the Pharaoh, He ordered all the newborn boys of my age group to be killed. I was spared when my mother placed me in a basket where I floated down the Nile to be found by the Pharaoh's daughter. I grew up surrounded by the splendor of Egypt, yet knew in my heart I belonged elsewhere. As a young adult, my anger placed me in trouble with the law, when I attacked a guard who was mistreating a slave, so I fled to the land of Midean where a devout family befriended me. I learned to become a shepherd, and started a family of my own. God truly blessed and protected me. I was content and thankful. Then I encountered God in a burning bush, He had a grandiose plan for me that was beyond my comprehension. He said, "Go to pharaoh and demand the release of the Israelites". "Who me?" "Yes, Moses, you!" Thus began a wonder-filled relationship with the one and only God who calls himself "I am". With my brother, Aaron, at my side we approached a pharaoh whose heart had hardened. There was no room for thanksgiving. One by one the plagues ravaged his land, yet he refused to let my people go. Pride and power were his gods and these relented to no one.

Then came the brutal, but necessary, night of Passover when our people were miraculously saved. Thanks be to God for our deliverance. All we had to do was believe and respond to that belief by smearing blood on our doorframes in order to be spared a horrible death. It is still the same today. Jesus is your Passover lamb whose promise of life is everlasting.

Now the great exodus began and I found myself in charge of two million people. To the shores of the Red Sea we fled, escaping through the sea itself. What a miraculous day! God's power was felt and feared. His mercy was palpable. We sang His praise and celebrated freedom in His name. Oh what a glorious memory. But reality soon slapped us in the face as the desert environment engulfed us in its bleakness. It did not take long for my people to forget their joy and thankfulness. The bickering had begun. "Oh that we were back in Egypt" they moaned. It escalated daily so I turned to God for help. He sent food from the sky and water from the rocks. A season of thanks returned. As we wandered further into the wilderness emotions ebbed and flowed between bouts of thanks and no thanks. Can you relate? It sure is easy to give thanks in times of bounty but God desires thanks in all things at all times.

As enemies were encountered battles erupted. None are as vivid in my memory as the great battle with the Amelikites. As long as I stood on the hilltop with my hands raised toward God we prevailed. When I lowered my arms we faltered. I have never been so tired in my life! But my friends, Aaron and Hur, helped me keep my arms up and we won the battle. Thanks be to God for His protection and the teamwork of my two friends. To this day God continues to protect His people. He has sent friends into your lives to help sustain your faith. Do these friends know how much they mean to you?

Still homeless in the desert we began to flounder. The newfound freedom was exhilarating but a void existed now that the Egyptian rule was absent. Imagine a society without rules, a people lacking moral direction, or a nation without etiquette. How are we to behave? Who will govern us? God boldly answered these questions on Mount Sinai via the Ten Commandments. These commandments are as relevant today as they were when I first brought them down from the mountain. Thank you God for your guidance and guardianship.

Guided by a cloud by day and pillar of light by night we wandered for 40 long years. Hardships abounded, grumbling emerged in waves of self-pity and disputes were as common as the desert vermin. Yet we held together for we had hope! A hope created by God. Without it we were lost. With it we moved forward toward the Promised Land. A home flowing with milk and honey, where we could build traditions, and praise our God. You too have a promised land. It was built by God, paid for by Jesus, and kept current by the Holy Spirit. You call it heaven—I call it home. Have you pondered the enormity of this gift? God wants to spend eternity with you! That must mean you are pretty important to Him.

My biggest disappointment in life was being denied entry into the promise land. My pride got the best of me one day and I disobeyed God, yet I thank him even for my punishment. Through it I had a constant reminder of who was in charge. As a result, I was a better leader and a wiser person. I was granted 120 years of life on this Earth. I stayed true to my word and close to God. I wasn't a superstar yet God accomplished great things through me. You too can be His agent. Be thankful for who God made you to be. Don't ask what should I change into; instead ask, "How should I use who I am to do God's will." God took me as I was and created a great leader, not by changing whom I was, but by molding me to fit his needs. I pray that you are willing to be molded by God. May you become great vessels; filled with hope, ready to do His will.

What do you hope for?

God Keeps His Promises

My name is Eli. I was a Hebrew teenager in Egypt when Moses burst on the scene to wage an incredible battle with Pharaoh in hopes of setting our people free. I was petrified as the carnage of the plagues swept over the city in waves of misery. Yet our people remained unharmed. The day Pharaoh finally said "Go" had to be one of the most joyous occasions in history. We danced—we sang— we packed. Freedom was ours and it was time to party. Our excitement made the first few days of the journey feel like a beautiful dream. Then came the Red Sea in front of us, and Pharaoh's army behind. Talk about a quick change of emotions. The festive atmosphere was replaced by fear. Hope turned to hopelessness, and brotherly love switched to bickering. Amidst the turmoil Moses calmly lifted his staff and God parted the sea. An incredible silence swept through the masses. Our God truly is an awesome God.

We as a people have probably experienced God's physical power more often than any others and surely tried his patience to Godly extremes. We complained about thirst – God purified our water. We complained about hunger – God sent manna. We complained about a lack of direction – God gave us the Ten Commandments. We worshiped pagan Gods – God forgave us. We doubted our success in the promise land – God gave us victory. Thankfulness was not one of our virtues.

We were a tough crowd to please and we paid dearly for our transgressions. I was nearly 60 before finally entering the Promised Land. But enter we did. God kept His promises and never left us. I marvel at the miracles bestowed on us and know in my heart we did not deserve them, yet God never gave up on us. I am forever grateful I chose to believe in the one true God.

Think about how you react during the ups and downs in your life. Would God ever leave you to rot in the desert of sin? No, He would not. I know first hand the depths of His patience and the power of his intervention. I hope you do too.

How would you rate your patience?

Encouragement

I am Mordecai. Looking back, I have come to realize my steadfast faith in God was a key tool in a complex drama that saved the exiled Jewish people in Persia. I am the uncle and adoptive father to an extraordinary woman named Esther. As Jews living in exile, we kept our faith at a private level. Esther's Hebrew name was Hadassah but she used it only around family. She was a beautiful young woman with a deep faith in God who viewed herself as ordinary. As it turned out Esther was anything but ordinary.

In a moment of rage, King Xerxes banished his queen and ordered a search throughout the kingdom for a new queen. Esther was taken into the harems of Xerxes and ultimately chosen as queen. Unbeknownst to him, King Xerxes now had a Jewish queen. Here is where the plot thickens. Haman, the Prime Minister of Persia, was a self-pronounced "Jew hater" who required all people to bow in his presence. I refused. Day after day I refused. This brave act could have put me in prison but I had earlier overheard an assassination plot on King Xerxes' life. When I relayed this information through Esther to the king, he was grateful and held me in high esteem. This buffered me from Haman's wrath. Hatred boiled within Haman as he vowed to get revenge by convincing the king to order all Jews in the kingdom killed. We were devastated when we discovered Haman had succeeded. I continued to refuse to honor Haman and knew in my heart that God would send someone to deliver us. I prayed daily for the salvation of our people. My God would not desert his people. Fully knowing she might be killed for approaching the king I encouraged Esther to speak to him. Esther confronted the king and revealed that she herself was a Jew.

To our delight, the king listened to Esther and reversed the decree, thus saving the Jewish people in Persia. I tell you this tale to encourage you. Stand firm in your faith and believe God will defend you against evil. Refuse to bow to false gods and He will reward your faithfulness. Encourage your friends to do what is right. We all fit into God's glorious plans. Pray for strength and trust in his guidance. He desires for you to succeed.

When was the last time you stood up for your beliefs?

Never Give Up

I am Joseph. As a child I was an overconfident dreamer who often flaunted my father's favoritism. This did not sit well with my ten brothers and triggered a life story filled with God's grace and protection. My adventures started when my jealous brothers sold me into slavery and told my father that I was dead. A fair man, named Potiphor, bought me at the Egyptian slave market and brought me to a new home in the palace of the Pharaoh. Through honesty and hard work I was elevated to chief slave in charge of his household. Life was good until Potiphor's wife falsely accused me of sexually assaulting her. Potiphor had no choice but to put me in prison.

Did I lose faith? No. In fact, the chief jailer soon noticed my skills and gave me authority over the other prisoners. Some time later, two personal attendants of Pharaoh were sent to our prison. Both of them had vivid dreams on the same night. The Lord granted me wisdom to interpret these dreams and they proved true. Two years later, Pharaoh himself was bothered by a recurring dream. The personal attendants who shared my cell told him about my ability. The next day I was summoned to Pharaoh's chamber in order to interpret his dream. The dream was warning Pharaoh of a massive famine to hit Egypt in seven years and included a plan to avoid disaster for this country. I was again put in charge of a household. This time the house was Egypt. I was no longer a slave or prisoner, but was second in command to Pharaoh himself.

I oversaw the storage of vast quantities of food during seven years of prosperity. The famine struck with a vengeance and left surrounding countries in dire need of food. This set up an unusual homecoming for me. My brothers came to Egypt in search of food and left with a greater appreciation for the grace of God. My story had come full circle. God had turned an evil act of jealousy into salvation for the house of Jacob. God used my strong faith and "never give up attitude" to orchestrate a chain of events that clearly underscored His power and His love. I could have given up many times, but He wouldn't let me. As a result, hardships turned into successes that benefitted His kingdom.

**Do you have a turnaround story,
where something seemingly bad turned into good?**

Faith Will Carry You Through

My name is Job. I was given much but also had much taken away. As I prospered I realized it was God who owned everything I had. It was He who gave and He who let it be taken away. Few people have experienced the ups I enjoyed and the downs I endured.

He had blessed me with great herds of animals, the service of hundreds of servants, and a wonderful family. I was one of the richest men in my area. Then everything was gone. In one fateful day, I lost everything. My sons, my herds, my servants— all were killed on the same day. Soon after, my health was attacked, and I cursed the day I was born. At first I thought I would be unable to withstand the onslaught of perils thrown at me, but I was wrong. My faith in God carried me through.

I mourned but did not blame. My friends said, "Get rid of your sin;" God said, "Be content." In the end, I weathered the trials and tribulations, and discovered the true meaning of contentment. God once again blessed my life with children, and gave me tremendous riches to manage. This time around I was at peace, and filled with the comfort of knowing God was with me. Would I do it again? I would not wish that on anyone, yet I know that my faith in God would carry me through.

When has faith helped you through a tough time?

True Faith

I am Mary. I vividly remember the day when an angel visited me with his amazing announcement. I was to be the earthly mother of our Lord! My emotions ran wild yet I was given the strength to say "yes". Me, a mother? I wasn't even married yet! If it weren't for my faith and the assurance that God was with me, I wouldn't have made it. I sincerely knew I couldn't do it alone. Joseph, bless his heart, supported and stood by me when I needed it most in those early days. Elizabeth and her miracle baby, John, also lifted my spirits. I was truly blessed and thanked God daily for His gracious gift.

After a torturous donkey ride to Bethlehem, reality hit. My son Jesus was born. The heavens sang out and wise men bowed, but it was I who had to change his diapers. Could I really handle this job God had given me? The answer came slowly as the years went by. Yes, I had the gifts to nurture my child. Sure I made some mistakes, like the time we forgot Jesus in Jerusalem. When we finally found Jesus he reminded me of whom he really was. You see, I had almost forgotten, because Jesus was so much like the other children in the village. When he started his ministry I had to give him back to God. It was hard hearing the stories of both miracles and murderous intentions while not being able to be at his side. Then it happened. He was arrested and crucified. This tore my heart apart, yet deep inside, God's original declaration gave me hope. Jesus was the Son of God and great things will be done on Earth through his actions. I wish I could say I knew he would rise from the dead, but I was too grief stricken to fully understand God's plan. Oh what a joy when I heard. My heart leapt just as it had done 33 years earlier. My son is alive and has returned to his father in heaven. Praise be to God! I often wonder why me? And I think I know the answer. I wasn't that special yet I had a special gift, the gift of faith. That faith and my unquestionable devotion allowed me to handle the task of raising Jesus. What does God have in mind for you? Trust me when I say, "Whatever it is, believe that He has given you the tools to complete the task." But don't ever get tricked into thinking you can do it alone.

When has faith helped you succeed?

Simply Amazing

I am David, son of Jesse, anointed by God through Samuel and friend of Jonathan. A redeemed sinner, I am the father of Solomon, and ancestor of Jesus. I am best known as a giant slayer but there is much more to my story than that. It is filled with twists and turns, ups and downs, but my steadfast belief in God's faithfulness and forgiving nature allowed this amazing story to bring good news to a world in desperate need.

I was born in Bethlehem the youngest son of Jesse. While not as tall or strong as my older brothers, I was gifted with a deep and sincere faith in God. God honored this by inspiring Samuel to anoint me as the future king of Israel at a very young age. In my youth I spent much time tending sheep and honing my musical talents on the harp. This skill brought me to the tents of King Saul a tormented man who found peace in my music. One of the sources of this torment was the Philistine army camped across the valley of Elah. Day after day they paraded out a giant named Goliath who taunted the Israelites goading them to fight. One day the power of God welled up within me as I proclaimed, " I will fight Goliath." I did, and God won the battle for us. It is simply amazing what you can accomplish with God's help.

I was invited into Saul's court and struck up a deep friendship with his son Jonathan. What a great friend. He knew it was I not him destined to be the next king, yet he did not allow jealousy to ruin his love for me. In fact it was Jonathan who saved my life when Saul went off the deep end and wanted to kill me. It is simply amazing what a friend can do to lift your spirits and keep you on track.

Saul was no such friend. As I ascended the ranks to become a successful commander, my fame spread. A jealous Saul flew into fits of rage. His contempt of me turned into a personal vendetta to kill me. So I ran. For years I wandered the wilderness with a troop of faithful men evading Saul's wrath. During this time I endured many hardships yet learned invaluable life lessons. I grew into a leader of men. It is simply amazing what patient resolve can teach us in times like these.

Following Saul's death I returned to Judah as King. Samuel's anointing those many years ago rang true. God had brought me to the throne. The kingdom was in turmoil; one war followed another as we built the kingdom God had promised. After many years Israel was finally one, and at peace within itself. There I was King of a mighty nation with God behind me every step of the way. Life was grand; I had made it to the top. It all seemed too good to be true. As it turned out it was. My sinful nature brought an abrupt halt to this utopia. Her name was Bathsheba, my sin—adultery. I compounded this sin with a worse one, murder. In an attempt to hide my liaison with the pregnant Bathsheba, I ordered her husband Uriah into harms way on the battlefield, in effect assuring his death. But it didn't stop there. I then took Bathsheba as my wife. Joy was soon replaced with sorrow, peace was replaced with depression, and my leadership plummeted in popularity as conspiracy reared its ugly head. The sword that brought me to power, turned against me as my family fell into turmoil. My life had gone from regal reign to rubble. God's consequences for my sin were dreadfully clear. Yet I was spared because I sincerely asked for forgiveness, and was granted it. God's grace is simply amazing.

Are you like me? It seems the better life gets, the harder it is to maintain your connection with God. Sin is always beckoning, waiting, nudging. The consequences of sin sometimes sting, and sometimes crush, but God is also beckoning, waiting, nudging. He wants you to mend your ways and sincerely call out for forgiveness.

My greatest accomplishments came after my death. Solomon, my beloved son glorified God as a mighty ruler using his gifts of wisdom and vision to lift God's holy name. He created a home for both Israel and our God; years later heralded by a brilliant star, an amazing gift arrived in a Bethlehem stable. God's ultimate fulfillment of covenants made with Abraham, Moses, and me. A boy with my lineage came into this world to spread the messages of love, hope, and peace. A new age was born through the sacrifice of this Godly man. His name is Jesus and he came just for you! A love that deep is simply amazing.

What words is He waiting to hear from you right now?

The Love of a Family

My name is Joseph, chosen to raise the son of man. I am a carpenter and grew up in the town of Nazareth about 65 miles north of Jerusalem. When Mary told me she was pregnant my simple life was shattered. By law I could have restored my reputation, by divorcing her on the spot, and having her stoned to death, but I loved Mary and believed her story. Instead of running away from the whole mess I stayed to become the father of her child.

The command to travel to Bethlehem for the census couldn't have come at a worse time. It was an eighty-mile trek and Mary was due any week. Despite the arduous journey and a filled up town with no space at the inns, Jesus was born and our family begun. Oh what a beginning. Visitors bowed down, the heavens shown bright, and love spread its arms around us.

Life in Nazareth wasn't easy, and the pressure on me to be a good father to Jesus was immense, but we made it through as a family. We valued each other, as we nurtured our faith in God. Jesus grew up knowing he was loved and loved us in return. I have often wondered why I was chosen and on many occasions felt the burden of my task. God, however, knew what He was doing. His love for us was evident through the beautiful child in our home. This gave me the strength and courage I needed to keep our family filled with joy.

**How much do you rely on your family
to help each other find joy in life?**

The Lamb of God

My name is Benjamin. As a follower of John the Baptist I often heard about the coming Messiah. The person John described as "the one who is far greater than I am for He existed long before I did. I am not even worthy to be his slave."

One day, while we were baptizing people in the Jordon River, John was reminding us of the one who would follow him and baptize with the Holy Spirit. Suddenly John's eyes lit up as his cousin Jesus approached. They greeted with a powerful hug and then John tensed as Jesus asked to be baptized. An unspoken excitement swept through the crowd. Could Jesus be the one? The answer came in dramatic fashion. The Heavens parted as the glory of God descended upon Jesus in the form of a pure white dove. An unearthly voice filled every crevasse in the valley with these unforgettable words. *"You are my Son, whom I love; with you I am well pleased."*

I glanced at John and witnessed a joy beyond description. Then it hit me. John's cousin Jesus of Nazareth was the one true God and John's ministry was coming to a close. John beamed from ear to ear as he rose to proclaim, "This is the Lamb of God!"

That night around the campfire we had some deeply intimate discussions during which John was able to convince me that Jesus, not he, was the one whom I sought. The next morning I bid farewell to my friend John and followed Jesus. My life has not been the same since.

**Have you been a John to someone,
and pointed them toward the love of God?**

Listen to Him

I am John, a disciple of Christ. For three years I encountered God on a daily basis as a follower of Jesus, yet through most of this time I didn't comprehend their full connection. The story that follows helped clarify it for me. We were resting in camp after a long day and were pretty tired when Jesus asked James, Peter, and me to accompany him up a nearby mountain to pray. This request wasn't that unusual but what happened at the top sure was. We settled in to pray and soon noticed Jesus' face begin to glow as if he had consumed the Sun. This breathtaking display heightened as Moses and Elijah appeared in clothes so dazzling white we had to shield our eyes. They stood there talking with Jesus as we sat frozen with wonderment contemplating the mystery of this beautiful sight. Suddenly, a cloud plunged the mountain into darkness intensifying the brilliance of the scene. Then it happened. Yahweh spoke in a voice that rumbled through our hearts with the strength of a thousand thunderclaps sending us to the ground too terrified to lift our faces. The words were clear "This is my beloved Son and I am fully pleased with Him. Listen to Him."

A few moments later Jesus touched my shoulder. I rose to find everything back to normal. He then said a very curious thing. "Don't tell anyone what you have seen here, until I have been raised from the dead." Don't tell? How can I keep this in? "Raised from the dead?" What does that mean?

I kept my promise and eventually came to understand that Jesus was the same God as the God we heard on that mountaintop. What an amazing sacrifice. God's whole time on earth was focused on me, you, and anyone else who believes in Him. Do you really comprehend the scope of God's sacrifice for you? He has risen from the dead, thus giving you permission to tell about your personal encounters with Him.

With whom have you recently shared your story?

Taking the Blinders Off

My name is Paul. What a difference a day makes! I am a man whose life changed overnight. My birth name was Saul. I grew up a devout Jew and student of the law. I was convinced in my heart that the Christians were a threat to everything we had worked so hard to accomplish the past several centuries. I thought I was doing God's work as I sought to destroy this new and dangerous religion. Then I literally saw the light. On my way to Damascus to round up Christians I was blinded by an encounter with God. He struck me down and left me blind. This encounter shattered my reality and replaced it with one of infinite joy, great adventure, and eternal hope. My eyesight was restored to see the true light, and my new name was Paul.

I had been wrong. I had gotten too caught up in the corporate nature of my religion. I had focused too much on the narrowness of the law. In short I saw the trees but missed the forest. Even though I had distorted truth and persecuted his people, God never stopped loving me. Instead he chose me to spread his word to many nations by telling them the gospel of His love. Was I worthy? Absolutely not! Was I willing? You bet I was! With God's help and the talents bestowed to me I was able to tell thousands about Jesus and spread his message of love and salvation. Sometimes we are blinded by personal ambition and corporate teachings. The only way to take the blinders off and see the full story is to humbly shed our ego and open our hearts to the love of Jesus the Christ. With His help I was able to put the pieces of my life together in a way that was pleasing to God.

Is your faith tied to a corporation or your heart?

God in My Heart

This is Paul again. After my conversion, God opened my eyes to the truth of His ministry and drafted me into His army, with the task of expanding His message beyond the Jews. His truth had set me free. My life goal had switch from persecuting Christians to spreading the good news that Jesus came to save all people who believe in him. God has been my protector every step of the way.

There was the time in Damascus when the Jewish leaders set guards at all gates in hopes of capturing and killing me. My friends were alerted to the plot and lowered me out of a window in a basket to safety. King Herod Agrippa imprisoned me, but amidst a flurry of prayer by my church, an angel led me out of jail. I was stoned and left for dead in Lystra but was healed and sent back to preach the next day. Silas and I were beaten with rods and imprisoned in Philippi only to be freed by an earthquake. I was shipwrecked on Malta and escaped death at the hands of Jewish leaders in Jerusalem because I was a Roman citizen. God literally never left my side. His joy was felt even in the roughest of times.

God did not waste any part of me as I spread the good news throughout the world. My biblical knowledge was used to connect the old ways to the new. My Roman citizenship allowed me privileges I wouldn't have had as an Israelite. My mind allowed me to solve complex issues relating to the acceptance of Gentiles. My ability to teach was used extensively. I met many great people and made deep friendships throughout the empire. These people strengthened my faith, took care of my needs and provided much needed support. But my true inspiration for ministry was an unfailing faith in Jesus as Savior and Lord. I had been changed from a person who knew about God, to a person with God in my heart.

What skills have you used recently to expand God's kingdom?

Joy in the Promise

My name is Thaddeus, one of the 12 apostles. Jesus trusted us to start His ministry. I am proud to say we succeeded. Over the span of three years we interacted with a diverse group of people, many of whom were frowned upon by the religious leaders. The Sanhedrin couldn't understand why Jesus would associate with tax collectors, lepers, and Samaritans. We grew to understand that Jesus offered salvation to all, not just the religious righteous.

Of the many highlights in our journey two really stand out. The first was when we were surrounded by thousands of hungry people on a remote hillside. Jesus said, "Feed my people" and we said "Impossible!" Boy, were we wrong! The second highlight actually happened twice. We were caught out in open water when gigantic storms threatened to drown us. The only thing that drowned was our doubts concerning His power.

We were a very human group of men, prone to weak moments. Peter denied him, Judas betrayed him, and we all abandoned him at Gethsemane. Remarkably, Jesus always forgave. Individually, we were at our weakest the first days following his crucifixion. If we didn't have each other's support, the ministry might have died with Him on the cross. But God wouldn't let that happen. Jesus rose from the grave and lifted our spirits to the sky! When he commanded us to spread the good news we heartily agreed. And then it happened. The Holy Spirit descended upon us and opened our hearts, awakening a mighty zeal to the full glory of God's plan. Halleluiah!

To say life was tough following his resurrection would be an understatement. Several in our group were put to death and all were persecuted. We endured because the joy in the promise was greater than the pain of preparation. We stuck together with bonds of deep conviction, buoyed by the Holy Spirit. Together we prevailed and managed to plant seeds of hope throughout the empire. Praise be to my master and savior. I pray that you too have the gift of fellowship to help you find joy in your journey.

Who do you go to for encouragement and support?

The Meaning of Messiah

My name is Peter, often referred to as the rock. But even a rock can be shattered by the power of words. Four little words spoken by Jesus shattered my pride and turned my faith upside down. We were walking away from Galilee tired after a long day. Out of the blue Jesus asked, "Who do people say I am?" We all knew the answer to that question but were afraid to say it. The repercussions of the truth were too great and downright scary. One disciple replied; "Some say John the Baptist," another said " Elisha;" and a third yelled out, "You are one of the other prophets." All were very safe answers. Jesus then looked directly into my eyes and asked: "Who do you say I am?" A knot formed in my stomach as I blurted out "You are the Messiah." Thankfully he told us not to mention this to anyone else. He went on to say that he would suffer terrible things and be rejected by the leaders. He said he would be killed and three days later rise again. This was not the way I envisioned the Messiah. I told him so, and he replied with those four words, words that ripped the ego out of my chest, and tore me apart. Jesus said: "Get behind me Satan." I turned away furious at being reprimanded. How could he call me Satan? I was loyal. I had been at his side for three years. I had given him everything I had … or had I? As I dwelled on his words a realization slowly crept into my brain. I had always viewed his teachings from a worldly perspective. He didn't seek to conquer this world. He sought to save it—one person at a time. Those four words shoved the meaning of "Messiah" down from my head to my heart. I finally got it. The pieces of the puzzle Jesus called salvation finally fit together for me, and my life became whole. I needed to turn my faith inward and make it personal. From that moment on I felt comfortable with the nickname of rock.

Is your faith in your head or in your heart?

Nothing Can Separate You
From the Love of Christ

My name is Judas. Yes I'm the one that betrayed Jesus. Yet my biggest mistake came after that traitorous act.

Let me take you back to the times of our ministry with Jesus. Of the 12, I was one of the most politically minded. At first I saw Jesus as an earthly savior, one who would take us out from under the bootstrap of the Romans and allow us to become our own nation. After all we were the chosen people. I was a pretty good businessman and often managed what little money we had. As we traveled Jesus seldom talked of money and often chided me for my continued focus on our economic welfare. Instead he focused on the welfare of our hearts. I never quite got to the realization that my heart was more important than my station here on earth. As a result I was an easy target for the Jewish leaders. Simply stated, I sold Jesus out. We needed the money and eventually Jesus needed to state his case in front of the leaders. I thought I was accomplishing both tasks in one bold move. Boy was I wrong. I was wrong about our needs and I was wrong about the true reason he was on earth.

I will never forget his face as he told me to leave the upper room and do what I had to. How did he know? And why did he look at me with sorrow instead of anger? As I turned him over to be arrested, shame ripped through my body from head to toe, but I was powerless to undo what was done. Then I made the biggest mistake of my life. On numerous occasions I had heard him say that nothing can separate me from his love. I didn't believe it. I had listened to his words, witnessed his miracles, and felt his love but I hadn't allowed His message to move from my head to my heart. Riddled with shame and aware of the enormity of my act I saw no way out but to kill myself. Yes betraying Jesus was a horrible act but one that would have been forgiven if I had truly believed in him. He could've helped me put the pieces of my life back together but I didn't allow him to try.

**Nothing can separate us from the love of God.
How do you interpret the word "nothing"?**

Living Water

You have never heard of me before and my name isn't important. Let's just say I was the guy who got kicked out of Adah's house. You may know Adah as the woman who met Jesus at the well. He knew everything about her, yet was compassionate and instantly befriended her. I was the last in a long line of men who casually shared her bed. She returned from the well a changed woman. She had a glow about her and talked of water that quenches spiritual thirst. She immediately asked me to leave and from that point forward worked hard on relationships. The glow that I mentioned never left her. Her self-esteem soared, as her life turned from drudgery to a downright delight. I couldn't help wanting some of what she had, so I asked her to share Jesus' message with me. My life too was changed. We began to court each other and took every opportunity to hear more of what people were calling the Good News. We eventually married and lived happily, basking in the knowledge that we will be together for eternity. Adah had given up on herself, but God had not. He sent his son Jesus so that people like us could reassemble the parts of our broken lives into the masterpieces God had intended. Beautiful creations filled with a peace that passes all understanding.

How often do you resist judging people?

Peer Pressure

I am a Roman officer named Marcellus. I grew up worshipping a group of Gods whose individual strengths combined to cover all walks of life. Headed by Jupiter and Juno, these Gods controlled every aspect of the Roman Empire. The Sun, the Moon, and the planets were named after them. Our Gods ruled even life and death. Caesar himself was deemed a God and demanded that type of respect.

I was stationed in Capernaum, a city filled with Jews who worshiped only one God. My household servants followed this "one true God" and they were the most trustworthy group of people I had ever encountered. Over time, I began to cherish their beliefs. When Jesus started preaching his message of love I was hooked.

When my head servant became deathly ill, I made a bold decision. I decided to approach Jesus on behalf of him. I knew my friends would ridicule me, yet still I asked some Jewish elders to approach Jesus with a request to heal my servant. To be honest I was surprised when I saw Jesus approaching my home. I rushed outside to stop him saying, "I do not deserve to have you enter my home. Just give the order for him to be healed and I believe it will happen." Jesus then spoke some words that will be engraved in my brain for the rest of my life. "I have not witnessed faith like this even in Israel." It was then I realized the Roman Gods of my birthplace had been replaced by the love of the one true God. When I returned to the bed of my servant I found him well and in good spirits. I am eternally grateful for my bold actions. My servant was cured and my faith was validated. Miracles happen. I personally know this for a fact.

Do your fellow workers know you are a "follower of Christ?"

Never Alone

My name is Romulus, a Roman centurion stationed in Jerusalem. One morning I was at my post near the home where a group known as the believers were staying. I had heard the stories of their Jesus who had been crucified a few months earlier, and witnessed the conviction of their belief in his resurrection. It was the Jewish feast of the Pentecost and the city was jammed with people. Twelve men were sitting in a circle deeply engaged in conversation when, without warning, a mighty wind roared through the courtyard. It was as if heaven had flung open its doors to dump its contents on the world. The sound was deafening. In the midst of this phenomenon, tongues of fire descended on the twelve believers and settled near their heads. These men seemed to swell with confidence and rose as one to prophesize.

Now here is the most amazing part of my story. I do not speak Hebrew, yet I understood every word these men were saying. Everyone in the crowd understood them no matter what their native tongue. I was perplexed and unable to move, seemingly frozen in time as a tingling sensation penetrated deep into my soul. People flooded into the square eager to witness this supernatural event.

A man named Peter assumed control of the situation and began preaching. He spoke of a long dead king named David who had predicted the coming of their messiah and laid out a convincing case for Jesus being this Son of God, who came from Heaven, sacrificed himself to cleanse us of sin, then returned to his place in heaven. The tongues of fire burned bright, comforting my soul and seemingly opening my eyes to this joy-filled story of a God who deeply loves all mankind, even me, a Roman gentile named Romulus. I was spellbound for hours and slowly came to the realization that my life was missing something. That something was the salvation freely offered by God. The next morning I, along with thousands of others, was baptized. I have never felt alone since. The comforting guidance of God's Holy Spirit has stayed with me throughout my travels as I proclaimed the joy offered by God through the good news of Jesus the Christ.

Have you encountered the Holy Spirit lately?

Together We Can Change the World.

We, the 12 disciples, were chosen by Jesus to spread His new gospel of love and grace. Why us? We certainly weren't educated world leaders or even men of high social standing. We were five fishermen, one tax collector and six men of other occupations. By earthly standards we were definitely ordinary. Jesus was making a statement right from the start of his ministry. He came to save all people. His ministry was not interested in social status or power. It was all about the status of the heart.

We disciples set everything aside to follow Jesus and approached our ministry with servant hearts. Peter, James, John, Andrew, and Philip turned in their nets to become fishers of men. Matthew left a corrupt life and became one of the first to accept God's grace. Bartholomew was a true fan who stood up for his beliefs. Thomas had trouble believing without physical proof, Jesus provided it and Thomas never doubted again. James and Thaddeus were not very outspoken, yet stayed faithful and dedicated to Jesus. Simon was a patriot willing to stand up and fight for righteousness. And Judas, unable to give up worldly desires, gave in to temptation. As individuals none of us stood out as world leaders, yet collectively we were able to get the world's attention by launching Christ's church.

You are just like us twelve, pretty ordinary by worldly standards, but extraordinary in God's eyes. He gave you talents to be used in furthering his kingdom. With help from your friends, you can change the world. Trust in your capabilities, and join with others to spread the good news. Expect great results when you join His team, because Jesus turns the ordinary into the extraordinary.

What have you done for God lately?

Life Trails of Wisdom

Letting Jesus be your guide

This chapter contains devotions written as if Jesus is speaking to you. Each one has a different topic, but all are based on the Gospels. These should be read when you are in a reflective mood, allowing time for His words to soak in.

May His voice speak to you.

Proverbs 2:6
"For the LORD grants wisdom!
From his mouth come knowledge
and understanding."

I Have You Covered

Based on the Gospel of Matthew

Come to me when you are tired and filled with stress, and I will give you rest. Receive my grace and let me help you. Remember this— I am humble and gentle, and offer rest for your weary soul. My love for you is perfect and will give you peace. I do love you. Oh, how I love you. You are perfect in my eyes, and like my father said to me at my baptism, I say to you now— you are my dearly beloved child, who brings me great joy. I created you in your mother's womb and I am pleased with who you are.

Know that I will be with you forever. There is a room in my father's house waiting just for you. It is true— whoever believes in me will have eternal peace. So do not mourn for the ones that have joined me— instead find joy in their final resting place. Live not for tomorrow but for today.

Listen to my voice and hear my teachings. *"Anyone who listens to my teaching and follows it is wise, like a person who builds a house on solid rock. Though the rain comes in torrents and the floodwaters rise and the winds beat against that house, it won't collapse because it is built on bedrock."* [1] I know there are pieces of your life that have broken off that bedrock and need reconnection. I offer you my help. *"Healthy people don't need a doctor—sick people do.... I have come to call not those who think they are righteous, but those who know they are sinners."* [2] Be patient and hold on to your faith. And so I tell you, never stop asking, for you will receive what you ask for. Never stop seeking, and you will find what you need. Never stop knocking, because my door is waiting to be opened. I do not tell you this to raise false hope. It is the truth, for I am the Lord Almighty and I can provide. Your life will be restored. Don't worry. Can worry add a single moment to your life, or change the outcome of any situation? Of course not! It can only eat away at hope, and hope is one of the most precious gifts I have given you. So trust in me and ask for healing.

If you think you have strayed too far to be helped— you are wrong! Remember I am the shepherd and you are one of my sheep. If you wander away, what will I do? I will leave the others on the hills and go out to search for you. When I find you, I will rejoice over this homecoming even more than I do for all those that didn't wander away!

I have some advice to help you live your life in a way that will bless both you and me. Make these two commandments your purpose statement. *"Love the Lord your God with all your heart, all your soul, and all your mind."[3]* This is the first and greatest commandment. *"A second is equally important: Love your neighbor as yourself."[4]* Live these and you will become the true light I intended for you. Yes, you are a light in this world. Let that light shine through good deeds, so that everyone will praise your heavenly Father.

In closing, remember:

I bless those who mourn, for they will be comforted.
I bless those who are humble, for they will inherit the whole Earth.
I bless those who are merciful, for they will be shown mercy.
I bless those whose hearts are pure, for they will see God.

I have you covered with my eternal peace. I have you covered with my unending grace and I have you covered with a love so deep nothing can separate you from it.

[1] Mt 7:24-25
[2] Mt 9:12-13
[3] Mt 22:37
[4] Mt 22:39

Matthew 28:20
"And be sure of this:
I am with you always, even to the end of the age."

A Call to Mission
Based on the Gospel of Luke

Peace be with you. Thank you for spending this time with me. Our relationship touches my heart, and brings forth memories of my apostles. I come to you now to affirm your earthly mission.

John paved my way, and then invited me to be baptized. At that moment the Holy Spirit filled me and cradled my heart with the warmth of my Father's love. I thank John for answering his call. Who has paved the way for you? Please thank that person for me.

Early in my ministry I asked three fishermen to follow me to become fishers of men. They responded by sowing seeds that bore much fruit. Can you identify a Peter, James or John in your life? Think of the potential they bring to my community. Invite them to join us. You need not worry about saying the right things. The Holy Spirit will teach you what to say. You are in my hands and I will not let you falter.

I pray your journey will be like that of Simeon. When he saw me, his mission was complete. He left with joy in his heart and sits with me now. My parents recited his words often to me as a child. I never forgot his declaration. May it also be yours: *"Sovereign Lord, now let your servant die in peace, as you have promised. I have seen your salvation, which you have prepared for all people. He is a light to reveal God to the nations, and he is the glory of your people Israel!"* [6]

Simeon built his house upon the rock of salvation. Have you done likewise? Deny yourself, join my team, and follow me. When you do this, your life will change. If you feel unworthy, put that behind you. I did not come to save the healthy— I came to help sinners become winners.

I do this not by putting a patch on old clothes. No, I make you new. A patch would just cover the tear in your life, giving a constant reminder of past failures. Instead, I clothe you in new garments and throw away the old. Wouldn't it be great to step into a new life and feel the warmth of my love surround you for eternity?

Cherish the community around you. Believe in its power to change the world. Remember, you are like yeast – unable to do much by yourself, but when combined with others, able to make great changes in the shape and texture of this world. I chose twelve to begin my new community. These twelve started my church and changed the world. What is your legacy? How many will join my community in Heaven as a result of your mission?

My mission was with me each day. *"The Spirit of the LORD is upon me, for he has anointed me to bring Good News to the poor. He has sent me to proclaim that captives will be released, that the blind will see, that the oppressed will be set free, and that the time of the LORD's favor has come."* [7] Know your mission and draw strength from my love for you.

My last words on Earth included a promise, and a call to mission. The promise is the gift of the Holy Spirit. The mission is to preach the good news to all nations. I thank you for spending this time with me, and have prayed to my Father to increase your faith.

The night of my arrest in Gethsemane, I asked my father for strength and received it. He helped me finish my mission. I bestow on you that same strength.

[6] Lk 2:29-32
[7] Lk 4: 18-19

As you invite others to join our journey of faith.
May your ears be open, your tongue be loosed, and your
actions bold. May you help change lives and strengthen your
community, from now until the end of time.

Amazing Love–Pass it On

Based on the Gospel of John

Peace be with you. I come to proclaim my love for you. My Father so loved the world He sent me so that everyone who believes in me will not perish but have eternal life. Do you believe this? I truly hope so. I long for the day when we can walk together in the presence of my Father.

While my greatest desire is for you to join me one day, please know my love is intended to bring you comfort and joy, not just in Heaven but also on Earth. I feel your pain as earthly events tear at your emotions. Know that I grieve with you in these times of trial. It would be much easier if I could guarantee a perfect life, but that's not the way it is. My Father created people with a free will so each may make their own choices. As a result, bad things happen to good people. It may not seem like a loving system, but it is. Instead of being a puppet with heavenly strings, you have the ability to take ownership of your life. It takes great love to let a child go, giving up that much control.

So try to be thankful in all things and know I am with you always to help you through any trial. I offer you a gift— peace of mind and heart. The peace I give isn't like the peace the world gives. Remember the story of the woman at the well in Samaria? I spoke with her of water that quenches a thirst, yet that thirst returns— it doesn't last. My peace does last. It is like living water, which becomes a spring continually supplying a peace that will quench the thirst of anything you may encounter. So don't be troubled or afraid.

While on Earth I performed many miracles, feeding thousands, healing, calming storms, and raising the dead. Yet my biggest miracle is you. You have sinned, and will sin again, yet I am so committed in my love for you I gladly forgive those sins each time you confess and ask for forgiveness. I realize you can't comprehend this forgiving act, so just accept it as a miraculous gift I lovingly offer.

So where's the catch? What do you have to do to receive all this love? It's simple. <u>Love me back</u>. When you love me as I have loved you, our relationship becomes real. You honor me by following my commandments, getting to know me through prayer, and studying my Word. I tell you the truth; if you love me, you in turn will be loved by my Father and by me. I will reveal myself to you and live within you. You will know this through the Holy Spirit who will teach and guide you through life.

When someone truly loves, they want to pass it on. I desire to have all people experience my love and ask for your help in reaching them. Go, therefore, and make disciples of the entire world. You have talents to contribute to this effort. Use them to love others, as I have loved you. Together we can do great things to make this world a better place.

Go now with the knowledge that I love you.
Nothing you can do will diminish that.
My capacity for love is amazing.
Feel free to accept it, and pass it on.

Encouragement

Based on the Gospel of Luke

Peace be with you. I come to bring you encouragement. An encouragement so immersed in love that my Father sent me as a sacrifice to save your life. I tell you the truth— you are worth every drop of blood I shed.

I know the comfort of encouragement and remember the times I was encouraged. For instance, as I came up out of the water after my baptism, the heavens were opened, The Spirit of my Father descended like a dove and settled on me. My Father's voice boomed forth with these words, *"This is my dearly loved Son, who brings me great joy."* [8] Confidence flowed through my veins and love filled my soul. Near the end of my mission as I faltered on the Mount of Olives, I prayed, *"My Father! If it is possible, let this cup of suffering be taken away from me. Yet I want your will to be done, not mine."* [9] At that moment an angel appeared to encourage me.

My mother also had stories of encouragement. At a time of great insecurity she asked "But how can I have a baby? I am a virgin." An angel replied, *"The Holy Spirit will come upon you, and the power of the Most High will overshadow you. So the baby born to you will be holy, and he will be called the Son of God. What's more, your relative Elizabeth has become pregnant in her old age! For nothing is impossible with God."* [10] She took this message to heart and joyfully accepted her role.

This same heavenly encouragement is available to you. For the great encourager, our Holy Spirit desires to be asked for help. He was there when I declared my ministry in a little synagogue as I read this scripture *"The Spirit of the Lord is upon me, for he has appointed me to preach Good News to the poor."* [11] He was there when my disciples started their ministry on Pentecost morning. He is also here right now, offering strength and support to you. Be encouraged and make the call. Whatever you do don't be afraid to act in my name, for I am with you always, and will not allow you to stumble. Be persistent like the men who lowered their crippled friend through a roof— and gain strength through my healing power.

Be bold like the centurion whose love crossed the boundaries of social pressure to save his servant— and experience the joy of my grace. Step out of the boat like Peter— and seek my comfort. Give like the young boy who donated a few loaves of bread and a couple of fish— and be fed. Work hard toward your goals like Noah— and experience freedom.

Never get discouraged. Instead, keep on asking, and you will be given what you ask for. Keep on looking, and you will find. Keep on knocking, and the door will be opened. For everyone who asks, receives. Once that door opens, my light will bring sunshine to your soul. If you are filled with light, then your whole life will be radiant, as though a floodlight is shining on you. Worldly situations seek to do just the opposite by tearing you down, but I tell you the truth. *God blesses you who weep now, for in due time you will laugh.*" [12]

So listen carefully to what I say. If you are open to my teaching, more understanding will be given, and if you understand my basic command, all else will follow. You must love the Lord your God with all your heart, all your soul, all your strength, and all your mind. Then, love your neighbor as yourself.

One sure way to love your neighbors is by encouraging them with a humble heart. Listen to their story without judgment— it will help them feel valued. Gently nudge them to open their heart— it may help them find a solution. Remember to call on my name, for if you acknowledge me publicly; I, the Son of Man, will acknowledge you in the presence of God's angels, then the spirit will descend to fill you with the gifts needed in that situation. So don't be afraid, it gives me great joy to offer you my kingdom.

[8] Mt 3:17
[9] Mt 26:39
[10] Lk 35-37
[11] Lk 4:18
[12] Lk 6:21

May my peace encourage your walk
so you can in turn encourage others.
In this way each of us can be a blessing to the other.

Amazing Love
Based on the Gospel of Matthew

Peace be with you. I come to you now to help prepare your heart for the great life we will share together. James and John left their nets on the shores of Galilee when I called out, *"come, follow me, and I will show you how to fish for people."*[13] They followed, and you are witness to their legacy. My disciples were ordinary men with extraordinary faith and determination. You have the talents to be like them. Hone the skills my Father instilled within you and continue the work I began those many years ago. Come be my disciples. I tell you the truth; going fishing with me is simply amazing.

Sometimes you think you're not worthy to follow me. Banish that thought right now! I have come to call sinners, not those who think they are already good enough. You are worthy. So worthy I came to Earth and sacrificed myself just for you. All people are sick due to sin, but you can come to me for healing. I thank you each time you visit, and forgive each time you repent. In my eyes you are simply amazing.

I often told stories that taught lessons. People with hardened hearts and icy souls saw what I did, but didn't perceive my meaning. They heard my words but they didn't understand. They did not turn from their sin and were not forgiven. Be proud that you are not one of them. One of my favorite stories involves soils. Seed was thrown on four different soils resulting in four different growth patterns in the plants. What type of soil have you been nurtured in? Was it hard-packed with little empathy, or shallow and materialistic? Was it filled with thorn seeds tempting you astray? Or were you blessed with rich soil surrounded by loving parents? Unlike a seed, you have the ability to change your growth patterns. Work with the soil you have been planted in. Soften your heart— and warm your soul with my fire. Hear my words— and understand I love you. Turn from your sin— and be forgiven. Become like the mustard seed— and blossom into a great person spreading my love. Spiritual growth can be challenging, but with my light providing the food, you can utilize any soil. You are destined to become a simply amazing creation.

I have performed many miracles, each intended to help people understand who I am, feeding thousands with scraps of food, walking on water, healing all sorts of ailments. Thousands were witness to my power yet many did not get the big picture because they were too focused on themselves. Anyone who wants to be first must take last place and be the servant of everyone else. *"For even the Son of Man came not to be served but to serve others and to give his life as a ransom for many."* [14] I still perform miracles today. They may not be as dramatic as those I personally performed and I often use people as my intermediary, but miracles they are. Don't just focus on the miracles. Look beyond them to this underlying truth. I am God— I exist and I am still present in this world. Believe it! Use this knowledge to gain courage and conviction to live a life pleasing to me. Remember— My power is simply amazing.

In my last week on Earth, I entered Jerusalem riding a donkey to choruses of Hosanna! I left crucified on a cross, then rose to spread my love throughout the world. On Thursday of that week I celebrated the Passover meal with my closest friends. During this meal I gave new meaning to the traditions of passing bread and drinking wine. I was preparing them for the new covenant. No longer would animals be sacrificed for forgiveness of sins. I was about to offer myself. The next time you prepare to commune with me, empty your heart of all grievances. Confess your sins and humbly repent.

Remember this. I, your Lord, am compassionate and gracious, slow to anger and full of loving-kindness. I have not dealt with you according to your sins, nor rewarded you according to your deeds. My love for you spans from Heaven to Earth and nothing can separate you from this love.

[13] Mt 4:19
[14] Mt 20:28

I am simply an amazing God.

All for One – One for All

I have waited since the beginning of time for this very moment. You set your busy life aside to spend this time with me and I am filled with joy at the sight of you. Who am I to be so happy with your presence? I am the God of Noah, Abraham, Moses and all the faithful of the Old Testament! I am Jesus your savior, who willingly went to the cross for you! I am the Holy Spirit who is present with you right now, willing to fill your heart with peace!

I am all of these and more. You need not bother trying to piece together the full mystery of my being, just believe in me, and know in your heart that your God, the Father, the Son, and the Holy Spirit love you deeper than you can ever imagine. I filled your world with intricate beauty— so you can experience peace. I came to Earth and suffered— so you can experience freedom. I am guiding your life— so you may become whole, as the beautiful creation I lovingly knit together into flesh and bone.

Know this, however, I will not manipulate your life or make decisions for you. Your free will is one of the most precious yet daunting gifts I bestowed on you. With it you can soar through a life filled with joy, or crash into the abyss of self-loathing. Either way I promise to never give up on you. You are always welcome to dwell in my presence. I never tire of your company, and am eager to spend an eternity proving this. There is nothing you can do to separate my love from you. Like the father of the prodigal son, I have great patience and an immense desire to welcome you into my loving arms.

I know you have had some very rough times in your life. I heard your cry of "Why me, Lord? How could you let this happen?" My very essence desires to reach out and fix these times, yet our love for you, prevents us from intervening. This is what I want you to know. I am the light of the world. Where I am there is no darkness. Trust in me and come into my light. Where I am there is no evil. Trust in me and feel my love. Life will continue to bring forth times of trouble. Decisions pull you away from me, accidents happen, addictions take hold, or sickness robs your health. In these times of sadness, look for me, seek me out, I will be there to bring you light, and hope, and peace of mind. Remember this, where I am, there is no darkness and there is no place for evil to dwell. I am your hope for a bright future. My peace will give you the courage to overcome the sadness, the fear, and the doubt.

My Bible is filled with inspirational stories interwoven with my grace, my forgiveness, and my judgment. These capture who I am. My grace is freely offered as a gift of love. Know that you are worthy of accepting it without reservation or expectations from me. When you accept my grace, you accept me, and our relationship deepens. My forgiveness as offered by Jesus is real. Just as my desire to spend eternity in your presence is real. My judgment is not intended to pour guilt or shame on your wounds, nor is it designed to establish a hierarchy. On the contrary, my judgment exists to bring you back to my side. I miss you when you stray, especially when you take on my role and judge your fellow man. I want to be in a loving relationship with each one of you. Love your neighbor as you love yourself and love me with your whole heart.

Seize this opportunity to enjoy my presence within you. I hope it reminds you of the beauty that surrounds your life. I trust you will find comfort in accepting the sacrifice I made for you. I desire peace for you as the Holy Spirit infiltrates your soul.

We as your God thank you for accepting all we have to offer.
Go in peace and Know that I am your God.

Trust in Me

Based on the Gospel of John

I come to you bringing my peace, but I do not bring it as the world does. I offer it freely with the deepest love— and no strings attached. Relax and soak in my words. Place all worry behind you— be not afraid— for if you believe in me, I will be with you until the end of times.

Trust in me – and enjoy eternal life.

Have faith in the gifts my father has knitted into your being. Use them to build strong relationships and further my kingdom on Earth. I tell you the truth! Whoever believes in me will do what I have done and even more. I have gone to the Father to secure your spiritual safety. I will do whatever you ask for in my name. My Father's glory, which shines through me, will also shine through you.

Trust in me – and spread your light.

In times of need I offer you the gift of the comforter, the Holy Spirit. Share this comfort with others by following my command to love one another. As I have loved you so you must love one another. Then everyone will know you are my child. Be friends to those in need and humbly serve, spreading peace and joy everywhere you go.

Trust in me – and receive my unending love.

Be not afraid of stumbling or fearful of saying the right thing. Stretch yourself knowing I am always right beside you. Don't let the burdens of life drain your creative energies. Have faith in your gifts for they are unique, molded to you and intended for good. Since you believe in me, streams of life giving water will pour out from my heart to be received by those you touch on your joyful journey.

Trust in me – and act on your faith.

"Know that I am the way, the truth, and the life."[5] I am the alpha and omega, the beginning and the end that joined you in Bethlehem, saved you on Calvary and entered your heart on Easter morning.

[5] John 14:6

Trust in me – for now and forever. Amen

And Jesus Said – "Go in Peace"

Peace be with you, and my peace I offer you. Many times I have joined with believers who realize they can't do it alone. I tell you the truth, those that accepted me as the true vine, have indeed born much fruit. Some of that fruit has fallen on fertile soil and became the seed of new lives. Some has brought immediate nourishment to feed the spiritually hungry. Be thankful for the servants that have planted seeds in your heart.

Know that with me at your side the path is perpetually lit for I am the light of the world. If you trust in me you won't have to stumble through the darkness of doubt, or the shadow of fear. Instead you will have the light that leads to life. Choose life, because I first chose you. Yes it's true; I did choose you, so trust in the gifts my father planted in your being. Use them for my glory with confidence that I will not let you stumble. Remember— it is I who is lighting your path.

If you team together with others in my name, nothing can extinguish the light that you will send forth. Find a friend, form a bond, and stretch each other. I tell you the truth, you will do even greater things because I have gone to my Father and His love for you is endless.

I leave you now in voice but not in spirit. For I have unleashed the Holy Spirit to guide and protect you. I chose you for a purpose and grant you the strength to discover that purpose. Go in peace, using my light to brighten your world.

**Go now in peace knowing that I am the vine
who is proud to claim you as one of my branches.**

Life Trails to Heaven

A joy filled journey
to the grave and beyond

This chapter was inspired by my beloved wife Carolyn Kranz who battled with breast cancer for over 15 years then passed away at the age of 58 on August 27, 2011. Her faith and testimony inspired hundreds, as she clung to hope and never let the disease beat her. Carolyn dubbed this experience as "The gift of Cancer".

These devotions are written from my personal perspective giving you a window into my soul during this journey. It is my prayer that you will be able to insert yourself into each story in a way that brings hope, as you contemplate the miracle of Heaven.

To give you a better perspective on the devotions in this chapter I have included Carolyn's powerful testimony given at Hosanna Lutheran Church on Valentine's Day, 2011.

If you would rather watch the video of this testimony go to: https://vimeo.com/19949696

The Testimony of Carolyn Kranz

Introduction by Dave Kranz:

Our story begins in 1970 when I walked into English 101 at North Hennepin Junior College and saw the girl of my dreams. Six months later I got up the guts to call her on the phone. I heard noise in the background and asked her about it. She was having a valentine's party. I was totally clueless. Three months passed before I asked her out, and another three months went by before I had the courage to kiss her. Despite dating two other guys at the time she showed extreme patience and my dream girl became my reality.

Married in November of 1974 we are the proud parents of two sons (Doug, age 30, married to Sarah, and Dan, age 25). In 1980, we joined this little church of 160 people in Lakeville called Hosanna! Here our faith journey blossomed. When we joined Carolyn said, "Don't expect me to get too involved." She had no idea what God had in store for her. She is an awesome pianist and God opened up an opportunity for her to play during the services. She is great with people, and the choir director position opened. She is organized and tuned into music trends; the director of celebration arts came into existence.

Between 1980 and 2003 as the music program grew so did Carolyn's relationship with God. Her God given talents exploded in glorious servant-hood once she accepted the challenge of using them. How about you? Have you identified your talents and put them to use? If you think you don't have much to offer consider this. In 1980 Carolyn was so self-conscious of her piano abilities she would not even play for my parents. The music at Hosanna that inspires us today is a result of leaders like Carolyn and a wealth of talented people who discovered their gifts and acted upon them.

Our most recent chapter in life started four years ago. I got some news followed by a comforting visit from the Holy Spirit. I arrived home from work to find out Carolyn had been taken to the emergency room with major back pains. She was still there awaiting an MRI. One hour later the phone rang with news that challenged my sanity and her health. Carolyn's breast cancer from eight years ago had returned with a vengeance virtually destroying two vertebrae as it wrapped itself around her spinal cord. Stage four-breast cancer — it's a death sentence.

On the way to the hospital, my mind was a blurry whirlwind of "what-ifs". There was a storm brewing in there so I decided to pray. The results were immediate. Faith kicked in. A tingling shiver leapt through my body. My knotted stomach relaxed and the racing synapses of my brain slowed out of warp speed. At that moment I knew God would take care of us and we would overcome this cancer.

I never dreamed we would be giving this talk in 2011. These past four years have absolutely been the best times of our lives. I love my teaching job like never before, we have taken more time to vacation, we have spent more time with family and friends, and our love for each other is indescribably delicious.

You see when you know time is limited you appreciate each moment more. **Here's the reality**. Time is limited for everyone. Once you view it as miraculous gift from God it becomes precious.

I have been blessed with the knowledge that God may call Carolyn home sometime in the near future. That may sound weird, but it is a blessing. I have already had four years of prep time to visualize, and come to grips with maybe finishing my life on earth without her. I do think about this often.

In the past 30 years Hosanna has offered many opportunities for me to build a solid faith. Nothing in my life has tested this faith more than the possibility of losing my dream girl. So far it has been a solid anchor. It wasn't always this strong. Remember that young man whom waited three months to call? I was an extremely shy person with low self-esteem. Three things contributed to building a trust in God. First I responded to the many opportunities Hosanna offered. Each time I said yes, God grew closer to me. Second my small group helped lift my self-confidence and most importantly, I came to realize "I am worthy of God's love". I pray that each one of you realizes that you also are worthy of God's love.

I'd like to end by reading an excerpt from the book "The Five People You Meet in Heaven" The main character Eddie has died and one of the people he talks to in heaven is his wife who died many years before him. The conversation starts with Eddie speaking.

"You died too soon. You were 47. You were the best person any of us knew, and you died and you lost everything. And I lost everything. I lost the only woman I ever loved."

She took his hand and said, "No you didn't. I was right here. And you loved me anyway. Lost love is still love Eddie. It takes a different form, that's all. You can't see their smile or bring them food or tousle their hair. But when those senses weaken, another heightens. Memory. Memory becomes your partner. You nurture it. You hold it. You dance with it. "Life has to end; love doesn't."

I am currently building memories so when the time comes for Carolyn to start a new life with Jesus, I will be prepared to carry our love with me until we meet again.

I proudly present "God's valentine present to me" — Carolyn Kranz.

Carolyn's testimony:

I need to take you back to 1998-99 when I was first diagnosed with and treated for breast cancer. There were three things I learned during that time that I refer to as "The Gift of Cancer". I opened that gift and this is what I found:

The first thing I found in that gift is that I did have the faith I thought I had. My faith had not been tested before and I always wondered if it would be there when a test came. When I found I actually did have faith in God, I felt like the cowardly lion in the Wizard of Oz, crying, "I DO have faith, I DO, I DO!"

The second thing I found in that gift of cancer was that the antidote to fear is TRUST. It came to me during the middle of the night before my first chemo treatment in November 1998 when I could not sleep. I was afraid. All I could think of were the possible side effects of this treatment. I would be sick. I would lose my hair. I would get mouth sores. I opened my Bible and it seemed that every verse my eyes fell upon had the word TRUST in them. Do I trust God in all situations or don't I? My answer is yes I do trust him. For me, where there is trust there is no fear.

The third thing I found in the gift of cancer 12 years ago was that it was important to allow people into my journey. This was certainly NOT my nature. My inclination is always to do it myself. I can do this. I don't need lots of people encouraging me, loving me. But I did. And there were many, many people who loved me. I was directing the choir at Hosanna at the time and there were about 80 choir members (well-known for being the largest small group at Hosanna!) who were the most loving people I've ever known. Remember back in the day David Householder talking about trying to take a sip of water out of a fire hydrant? It was HARD to accept all that love. Was I worthy of it? What would I do with it? Then this realization hit me:

If I turn these people away—if I do not accept their love— it would be the same as turning God away. After all, WE are all he has on this earth to do his work. He gave us the Holy Spirit and he gave us each other. If WE don't do his work, who will? I had to believe that these loving people were being Jesus to me. By allowing people into my journey, I allowed God into my journey.

So those were the big takeaways from 12 years ago; faith, trust, and people.

Eight years went by. I became part of the world of "cancer survivors". I was thankful for my complete healing.

Then February 1, 2007 came. I had been experiencing severe discomfort in my back and left work early the day before. My boss called me on my cell phone on the morning of February 1, to see how I was doing. I talked to him while sitting on the stairs in our house. After the call, I could not move. Our younger son Dan was home. I yelled for him to help me but his bedroom door was shut and he could not hear me. I called his cell phone from my cell phone and off we went to the emergency room.

This is where things get exciting! I was in a curtained partition in the ER where they were trying to get an IV into me to ease the pain. It's hard to get into my veins so they called in the special team of IV people, but they didn't come and they didn't come. I did not know how I was going to handle this pain in the meantime. Then it occurred to me:

I can pray! Duh! I visualized Jesus on the cross in excruciating pain. I asked God who had taken the pain and sin of the world on his shoulders for me and for you – I asked him to take away my pain in Jesus' name. The pain was gone. It left my body. Knowing God was right there to answer my first prayer gave me courage to face whatever was going to come next. God and I were partners now. The special IV person came and did her thing and I was ready for the tests.

The tests showed a major tumor wrapped around my spine. It had damaged one of the vertebrae to the point of collapse and that is why I was in such pain. And it is why I am now more than two inches shorter than I used to be! The tests showed several other tumors up and down my spine and in my pelvis. So now we know this breast cancer has metastasized which puts you in Stage 4 cancer. It is terminal. Because I am the Queen of Denial, I didn't really buy into the terminal part very seriously. I did know, however, that this was a fight that was going to be fought for the rest of my life.

We called our older son who now lives in Racine, Wisconsin, to tell him the news. His first question was, "Why is it always YOU, Mom?" My response? "Why NOT me? I can DO this!"

What would ever make me think that I am so special that I am going to be spared anything challenging? So I didn't wonder "Why me?" Instead, it was "Why NOT me?" I figured this would become an opportunity for me to show what God can do in a scary situation. How would that happen?

I was in the hospital for a week. I asked Dave to bring my Bible. I was in Philippians. Four words danced off the pages of Philippians.

It became clear that I needed to adopt four phrases from Philippians and live by them. These are my four phrases for life.

I will be joyful.
I will be thankful.
I will be prayerful.
I will be humble.

I shared those four things with my nurse. I shared them with all the people who visited. I wrote thank-you notes with them. I asked people to please pray those four things for me. I promised myself that if there came a day when I found myself feeling sorry for myself, or fearful or angry – that I would say those four phrases and see if they didn't turn me around. I will be joyful; I will be thankful; I will be prayerful; I will be humble. They have never failed. They have NEVER failed. I think that's a miracle: God led me to Philippians. I saw those words. I chose to adopt them as my own. They gave me life. They GIVE me life.

Was that the only miracle? Oh no. No way.

There's a kind of doctor called an oncology radiologist who studies your tumors and determines what radiation is best for your case. He brought me into his office during one visit to show me some very vivid pictures of my spine and the tumors on the spine. He called the major tumor "troublesome". We could not continue to radiate it without damaging the spinal cord and eventually becoming paralyzed. Then he told me about a machine that was being installed. They had waited 18 months for it to come from Germany. They had researched all the machines of this type and they settled on this one, called the Novalis. It would be able to radiate my tumor without affecting any tissue on its way to the tumor. It would not affect my spinal cord – only the tumor itself. It is programmed to within one millimeter of accuracy to radiate ONLY the area you want radiated. Sign me up!

I was the very first person to have the Novalis used on the spine. Channel 4's Dennis Doda did a little segment on the Novalis and they used me as the patient. Methodist Hospital put me on the cover of their monthly pamphlet, highlighting the new Novalis machine. That machine is now used 24-7 for all types of tumors. The miracle for me is that it was installed and ready to go the week I needed it. I am a thankful person.

Then they told me I would need to wear a brace for three months. I will show it to you. I now have abs of steel! Or plastic – or whatever this thing is made of. I wondered how I would ever wear this for three months. It affects what type of clothing I can wear. It makes it impossible to tuck a shirt in. It is a bit claustrophobic. It weighs four pounds. I sweat underneath it. I have to take it off every time I go to the bathroom, every time I change clothes. There's really nothing attractive about it. But guess what? It is my best friend. It keeps the winter winds from reaching my body. It keeps the summer sun from reaching my body. Most importantly, it gives me the strength in my back that the cancer has taken away. And I can sit at the piano in comfort. Playing the piano is my worship time and my prayer time. Well, three months of wearing the brace has stretched into almost four years. What I thought would be impossible became something I live with daily.

How did that happen? First of all, I had to believe that God could do anything – even turn this monster of a contraption into a good thing. So I made a decision. I would NEVER complain about this brace. Ever. What good would it do? And the truth pretty much is that I have never complained about this thing. It is good.

Chemotherapy started right away. To make a 4-year-long story short, just let me say that I decided to enjoy my treatments. What was the alternative? Dread them? They came around all too often to dread them. So I decided I would dress up for my treatments and make them the highlight of my week.

My oncologist, Dr. Duane, is marvelous as is all the staff at the cancer center. I have my favorite Nurse Nancy. We do a lot of chatting. She is interested in the lessons I am learning. At my treatment last month she asked me, "What were those four phrases again?" So I told her. I will be joyful. I will be thankful. I will be humble. I will be prayerful. She said, "Oh yeah."

I am treated like a queen at my treatments. The treatments have been extremely tolerable. I hardly ever experience the sickness many people do. I do not experience mouth sores. I was able to work full time. Other than for treatments I never took a sick day. How can I explain this? I can't. But God can. For me, it is a miracle. I am a thankful person.

It was the night after Easter last April when I had a heart attack. Well, this was a new adventure for me! I called the emergency 24-hour number. While I waited for a doctor to call me back, my discomfort was intensifying and again I didn't know what to do. Duh! I could pray! This time I prayed by singing a verse and refrain of "How Great Thou Art." The pain left my body immediately. Again, God and I were partners. When they put a stent in they saw that I have a mass in my right atrium. It is a mysterious mass. Thinking it was a blood clot; they put me on a blood thinner for a few months. In August they checked to see if it had dissolved— nope, still there. Also in August we found that the cancer had spread to my liver. So the heart surgeon, though he'd love to do open-heart surgery to remove this mass, said, "You have cancer in your liver. I wouldn't do the surgery." Now I realize I could die two different ways: From the cancer or from a piece of this mass in my heart breaking away and killing me instantly.

In September Dr. Duane asked me what measures I was willing to go to prolong my life. I told him I am not interested in any drastic measures. I am ready to go if we have used up all of our options. So I asked him why we're talking about this now. Do I have less than a year? He said, "Probably so."

I have had to ask myself many times since that talk with Dr. Duane, "Do you trust God or don't you?" Of course I do. That knowledge alone removes the fear. Am I sad that I will be leaving Dave and our two precious boys? I cry every time I think about it. Do I want my 90-year-old mom to outlive her youngest child? Of course not. It's her biggest fear. But will I allow God's light to fade and the darkness to overcome it while I wait for the end of my life? Absolutely not.

This Fall Dave and I have done some business. We've put our finances in order. We've had the legal papers drawn up for our Will, Health Care Directive and Power of Attorney. We've talked about a memorial service, cremation. I quit working so I could simply enjoy my days and connect with people. All of a sudden, the only thing important to me is people and relationships. This is why:

As I contemplate Heaven, I'm pretty sure there's a lot of love there. Tons of it. Where does it come from? I believe we bring it with us. I believe we get to take all the love we have for others and that they have for us. And we get to meet up with the love that preceded us there. Love from the people who've gone before us. We reunite with all of that love. I want to take a boatload of love with me. So it's important that I do a boatload of loving while I'm here.

See? Knowing that the end of my life is perhaps within the next year is a gift. I have been given the two-minute warning. I get to pull out all the stops. I get to love more. I get to prepare. I get to use my time with people rather than work.

When my friends want me to explain the peace I feel, I get to tell them. I tell them that I have the best antidote to fear – and it is Trust in the Lord. I get to tell them that I made a promise to myself four years ago that I would live the words of Philippians to be thankful and joyful and prayerful and humble. When they want to know why God isn't answering their prayers for me for healing, I get to tell them that I believe God is absolutely answering their prayers. I am pain-free when I should be in pain. I have hardly any side effects from the chemo when I should be sick and tired. I truly enjoy having no hair. You might think it's the chemo that makes my hair look like this. Wrong. I keep shaving it because I like it this way! God has for surely answered prayers for healing.

And He has given me a husband who is so totally on the same page as I am with his faith. I don't have to drag him along and reassure him every day that I really am fine. He believes me when I tell him I'm doing well. I believe him when he tells me he is going to be able to cope when I am gone. He has never made me feel less than beautiful – through reconstructive surgery and, believe it or not, he likes me with no hair! He's always thinking of ways to make my weeks fun and enjoyable. We have the time and the desire to talk about all sorts of things. And then there are my boys. My boys. I can hardly go there because I love them so much. They are so loving and they show it to me. They tell me. We tell each other "I love you" several times a day. We have the opportunity now to make some terrific memories. It's fun and our time together is rich.

At my treatment in December, Dr. Duane was making small talk and asking me how my Christmas preparations were going. I said they're all going fine, but I find it hard sometimes to reconcile in my mind that I won't be here for another Christmas. His immediate response was, "Then STAY!" He said they as doctors can only do their best to assess what is happening to the body physically. But he said they don't know anything about the spirit. He said, "Carolyn, you have such a huge and wonderful spirit. I believe that spirit is going to take you far."

So I live with such hope. I hope to hold a grandchild some day. And I live with a promise. We who believe that Jesus is our Lord and Savior are promised eternal life. So whether I live here and make more memories and see a grandchild and learn more and love more – or whether I die tomorrow, I have that wonderful promise. The promise of life after physical death gives me peace.

In the words of our dear sweet Hosanna friend Peter Erickson, either way I win. It's a win-win kind of thing. Every day on this planet is a gift. Every day brings me closer to the promise of a life forever in heaven. It is the same for every one of us.

My fear in telling all of this to you is that it would sound like it is so easy for me. I have my act together. I never had to wrestle with anything. But here's the deal. This is simply my story. The story of God working in me throughout my life. It is looking back at his faithfulness in the past 58 years. Despite my human-ness, despite the fact that I have been less than perfect, despite disease, God has loved me. I was in my 40's before I realized God loves me no matter what. I believe it is in accepting His love for you and finding yourself worthy of His love that you find peace in your life – no matter what the circumstances.

I guess that's what I want you to take away more than anything. God loves you. He knows you. He made you. There is nothing that can separate you from His love. Not life. Not death. Isn't that good? Isn't that the best?

It makes me thankful.
It makes me joyful.
It certainly humbles me.
It causes me to pray with thanksgiving all the time.
Thank you, God!

The Gift of Cancer (Carolyn's Story)

Written by Keith Mattson after hearing her testimony.

It came at first with lessons that I would not waste:

> It taught me that my heart was true,
> > And confirmed to me my faith.

> It taught me life is precious,
> > So enjoy it while I can.

> It taught me to accept the love
> > Poured out to me by friends.

> It taught me to reject the fear
> > And lean on Him in trust.

And I know I'll be in heaven when this body turns to dust.

It came back again years later to see if I had learned
The lessons taught, or had I forgot? Or had the fear returned?

But my faith is strong, and I still rely on Him in trust.
The cancer spread, but I said, "I will do this if I must!"

So I choose to be THANKFUL, & I don't question what I've got.
I choose JOY, & I choose PRAYER & I HUMBLY say, "Why not?"

I won't complain about the love that I've been shown.
I won't complain about the body brace I own.
I won't complain about the simple hairdo that I wear.
I won't complain "Why me?" or claim life isn't fair.

I WILL BE THANKFUL. And His praises I will lift.

**I am so amazed by grace and joy,
and that this cancer was a gift.**

An Angel on My Doorstep
(Written during Carolyn's last week on Earth)

I have an angel on my doorstep, who asks to come on in.
I hesitate to answer, not knowing where to begin.
Should I be joyful and full of praise? Or fearful of what's to come?
Who am I to question? My brain is rather numb.
I know that she is bound for heaven, fears just do not fit.
Yet I am human and feel the need to mourn a little bit.

I have an angel on my doorstep I am ready to welcome in.
When the time is right, and she has to go, we both will surely win.
For Carolyn will be in heaven worshiping with God
And I'll be here on Earth feeling kind of odd.
Yet we will be together, bound by one true love,
Comforted and held by God and His holy dove.

I had an angel on my doorstep, who came and took her home.
He gently swept her off her feet, to heaven they did roam.
I look around and start to frown for she's no longer here.
Then I realize where she is and peace drowns out the fear.
She is with God, and lots of friends, her new life has begun.
Thank you Lord for conquering death through your beloved son.

There was an angel on my doorstep, who shielded me from harm.
She was joined by many friends, reaching out with loving arms.
We had a celebration of life, the best in many years.
The Holy Spirit filled the room, bringing peace and joyful tears.
 Worship, talks, & sweet-sweet songs caused hearts to nearly melt.
We honored Carolyn, and our dear Lord, their presence surely felt.

The angel has left my doorstep, yet I am not alone.
For God still calls me by my name, I hear him from his throne.
My mind is filled with pleasant memories, waves of sweet relief.
I know her love is with me still; its peace consumes my grief.
Life moves on at a different pace, the wreckage under repair.
I miss her often and want her back, yet hope drowns out despair.

I give her now to you oh Lord with Thanksgiving for your gift.
Knowing she is in Heaven with you, gives me a great big lift.

Eternal Thanks

Have you ever pondered your interview with God on judgment day? The scene may go something like this: "Welcome John, I've known you since time began and am so pleased you decided to share a close relationship with me. You have truly become the creation I intended and the world is now a better place. The evidence is strong. You are my child! Before entering the full glory of my home I would like to hear your perspective of your time on Earth."

I would respond, "Thank you Lord! It was hard to grasp the reality of this interview, but by faith I always believed it would happen. My life has been blessed through our relationship. You picked me out of the dirt when I stumbled and freed me to really enjoy the good times. The community provided by your family was a needed anchor in times of trouble and became a treasured part of my life. It kept me sane and focused. Your grace, as we say on Earth, was a Godsend. I never was able to become sin free yet was freed each time I asked for forgiveness. My times in prayer with you were highlights of many days and that feeling you gave when we partnered, literally sent shivers through my spine. Because of you, many of my friends will be joining us. Thank you for choosing me. The joy I experienced on Earth will become insignificant to what lies ahead. I believed and am now ready to be received."

The question of the day is simple. Could you substitute John's name for your own? It's never to late to receive God's promise. Simply believe it's true, ask for forgiveness, start a relationship, and get ready to say "thanks" for the rest of eternity.

John 14:2
"There is more than enough room in my Father's home.
If this were not so, would I have told you that I am going to prepare
a place for you?"

Miracle Cures

Several years ago I arrived home from work to the news my wife Carolyn had been taken to the emergency room with major back pains. She was still there awaiting an MRI. One hour later the phone rang with news that challenged my sanity and her health. Carolyn's breast cancer which we thought was gone had metastasized and virtually destroyed several vertebrae as it wrapped itself around her spinal cord.

On the way to the hospital, my mind was a blurry whirlwind of "what-ifs". Midway to the hospital I talked to God. There was a storm brewing in my mind that needed calming. My faith kicked in as a tingling shiver leapt through my body. My knotted stomach relaxed and the racing synapses of my brain slowed out of warp speed. At that moment I knew God would take care of us and we would overcome this cancer.

We were about to witness one of three types of miracle cures. The easiest to handle would be an outright purging of the cancer. It happens and God can do this. Another cure resides in the miracle of medicine. New treatments and medications make this type of miracle more common each day.

The hardest cure to accept as a miracle is death. This however, may be the boldest miracle of the three. When Christ sacrificed himself for us, He promised heaven with all its beauty. Believing in Him gives us hope in the midst of pain. Knowing that heaven awaits helps wipe out the why's, wilts the worry, and washes the "what ifs" away.

Now that she is gone, I realize there is a fourth miracle cure. At His last supper Jesus broke bread, gave it to his friends, and said "Take and eat, this is my body shed for you". As the bread was shared, so was Christ's love. The miracle is this. As the body of Christ rallies around each other, all are healed. Life is different now but my faith remains strong. Each new day dawns with hope painted in the sky. Thank you Lord for miracle cures.

John 3:17
"God sent his Son into the world not to judge the world, but to save the world through him."

Little Words – Big Benefits

My wife Carolyn is battling metastasized breast cancer with the help of four little words: joy, prayer, thanks, and humility. Each of these has cultivated big benefits for her and the people around her.

By focusing on the positives in life (which are more numerous than most of us realize) Carolyn has found joy everywhere she looks. Her friendships have deepened, especially the one with Jesus who is but a thought away. Prayer has become more personal and pleasurable as she reaches out to Him for comfort. She relates one story of lying in a dark hospital hallway on a hard gurney with excruciating back pain awaiting an MRI. Suddenly she realized "I could pray about this!" and does. Both mind and body relaxed to make this scary situation bearable.

Because she is thankful for her relationship with God, Carolyn has been able to avoid asking "why me?" I discovered her thankful heart is contagious. While Carolyn was on the phone in the hospital, her roommate waved me over. She pointed to my wife and said, " I'll never ask "why me" again. Every time she talks to someone she is so positive and full of thanks that it has made me realize a negative attitude brings only harm." Daily life with positive people is positively joyful.

Carolyn views humility as the underlying theme that anchors the other three. "We are not here to serve ourselves but to do God's will." When life is viewed through these lenses it takes in a new vista that focuses on the life around you: not just the life in you. Whenever Carolyn begins to get unbalanced she repeats these four little words: joy, prayer, thanks, and humility. Life realigns itself to what God intended for her: A prayer filled life, of joy and thanksgiving, powered by a humble heart. What are your four little words?

Philippians 4:4-6
"Always be full of joy in the Lord. I say it again–rejoice! Let everyone see that you are considerate in all you do… Don't worry about anything; instead, pray about everything."

Self-esteem

I grew up with very little self-esteem. That has changed due to the growth in my faith nurtured by my church, and Carolyn's "gift of cancer". As I came to understand God loves me "the way I am". I no longer wasted energy trying to please people. Instead I focused my energies on honing the skills He instilled in me. Suddenly it dawned on me that I truly am a person wonderfully made by His hand. I was stitched together by a loving God who makes no junk. What a self esteem builder!

When Carolyn's cancer first appeared, the floodgates of love opened, soaking me to the core. It felt as wonderful as an open fire hydrant on a 100-degree day. Then came round two. Friends opened their hearts and taught us how to receive. As we were settling in to the new reality that Carolyn's cancer had returned, my principal at Eagan High School interrupted lunch with an envelope. Inside that envelope was money collected from my colleagues to send Carolyn and I on a cruise. (Can you say, "Wow"? I sure did.) Through these people, I was reminded that I indeed was wonderfully made.

It is very difficult to learn the art of receiving, but it sure was fun practicing.

Today I am a better teacher, a better husband, and a better friend with much higher self-esteem. I know I am loved—by God, by family, and by friends. Believe it when God and your friends say, "I love you." Then receive the gifts of grace and friendship, to fill your self with esteem.

Psalm 139:13-14
"You made all the delicate, inner parts of my body
and knit me together in my mother's womb.
Thank you for making me so wonderfully complex!"

A Match Made in Heaven

Too many times we take for granted the people in our lives. What would our trials be like without their helping hand and friendly smile? How much impact do they really have on our outlook of life? Carolyn had several relationships that could be classified as matches made in Heaven.

For the final 13 years of her life her oncologist was Dr. Stephen Duane. The mutual respect between Dr. Duane and Carolyn led to a relationship that borders on family. Carolyn always looked forward to her appointments despite the fact each one included nearly four hours of chemotherapy. His gentle spirit, coupled with her positive attitude turned a potential nightmare into the journey she called a gift. Three months before Carolyn passed Dr. Duane announced he was leaving to head the hospice program. This was exactly the time chemotherapy was no longer working and Carolyn had to enroll in hospice; the very same program Dr. Duane was now heading. They finished the journey together. Thank you Lord.

Carolyn and I were blessed with many friends who never let us feel alone. We had parties, visited their cabins, sat around the campfire, and shared life together. This helped lift our spirits to allow the joys of life to overshadow the thoughts of death.

As we travelled this journey together, our faith made us a match from Heaven. It tempered the highs and lows to smooth out the bumps along the road. Our mutual support of each other was critical in keeping us emotionally healthy and spiritually fit.

Who has God placed in your life to help make your journey the best it can be? These matches can ignite a zest for life that brightens your path today, tomorrow, and forever.

Ecclesiastes 4:9-12
"Two are better than one, because they have a good return for their labor: If either of them falls down, one can help the other up. But pity anyone who falls and has no one to help them up."

As I Contemplate Heaven

After the breast cancer was confirmed both Carolyn and I contemplated the mystery of Heaven quite often. What's it really like there? How long is eternity? Is there a physical part to heaven? These and many other questions popped into our heads and gave us food for thought. Neither one of us however, questioned its existence. The comfort of knowing Heaven exists, and God walks with us were ever present throughout Carolyn's journey. This assurance brought us much peace and kept the fear meter in the safe range.

For me, heaven is best represented by the peace that Jesus often referred to as "beyond understanding". I believe we will fully understand His peace in heaven. Imagine being in the presence of God surrounded by loved ones without physical limitations. That is total peace, and that to me is heaven.

About a year before she passed Carolyn gave her testimony at church, which included this vision of heaven. "As I contemplate heaven. I'm pretty sure there is a lot of love there, like tons of it. Where does it come from? I believe we get to take it with us. We get to take all the love we have for other people and all the love they have for me, and we get to meet up with all the love that is already there. Then we are reunited with all that love. Well, I want to take a boatload of love with me – so I have to do a boatload of loving while I'm here."

Both of our concepts of heaven are anchored by words that Jesus used often: love and peace. These actions helped bring Heaven to Earth. As we love others and come to peace with ourselves we bring little bits of Heaven down to Earth. What is your vision of Heaven? And how can this vision be incorporated into your actions before you get there?

Psalm 136:26
"Give thanks to the God of heaven.
His faithful love endures forever."

Down the Up Staircase

Did you ever play the opposite game, where up means down, yes means no, and in means out? Here is a possible scenario for this game. Instead of referring to deteriorating health as going down, let's call it going up. If we frame the dying process in the context of moving toward heaven, then each physical step down is a spiritual step up. By looking through this lens we keep the focus on God and diminish the earthly realities of the disease. The real reality is this: We are on this earth for a limited time. When this time draws to a close a brand new world is ushered in. A world beyond our imagination, filled with joy, peace, and love. A world promised to us by God, and delivered to us through his son Jesus Christ.

As our earthly body begins to fail, our spirit begins to soar. I witnessed this as my wife slowly withered away. Her body became weaker; her mind became more jumbled; yet faith stuck to her like superglue. She showed no fear and exuded peace right to the end. The sadness of leaving this world was balanced by the excitement of an eternal journey to Heaven.

It is like a glass holding half the liquid it is capable of. Is it half full, or half empty? Too often when death approaches we view that glass as half empty. If we view the glass as half-full, then fill it with hope, God will be sure to lift us up.

I am going to fill my glass with eternal hope. A hope that the physical ride down will end as a spiritual ride up. I will then ascend like an eagle to infinity and beyond.

2 Corinthians 5:1
"For we know that when this earthly tent we live in is taken down, we will have a house in heaven, an eternal body made for us by God himself and not by human hands."

Turning Downers Into Delights

One of the most intimate moments of Carolyn's journey occurred in our dining room. Her hair was thinning due to the chemotherapy and she asked me to cut it all off. The cancer was here and there was no way to hide it. We could no longer deny the reality of her situation. Both of us added tears to the hair falling to the floor. However within a week she discovered the joy of not having to fix her hair, and the fashion world of hats. Her attitude had turned a downer into a delight.

After the cancer had weakened her vertebrae, Carolyn was fitted with a body brace. A river of tears flowed in the car on the way home from the doctor that day. How can she dress and look good with this monstrosity surrounding her from shoulder to waist? Her fashion conscious life appeared to be at an end. The next day she made a decision. "I will not let this body brace ruin my life." Over the next few months she discovered ways to accommodate the brace. Eventually she referred to her brace as her "abs of plastic", and protector from cold winds. This downer supported her broken spine and allowed her to continue life in pain-free manner. What a delight!

In these and many other situations she had adopted an attitude of gratitude and it rubbed off on me. Several times in the last months of her life Carolyn thanked me for supporting this attitude. If your partner has a positive attitude and you don't; just "fake it until you make it." That way both of you can feed off each other's emotions in a positive way. We have a choice: to be angry for the time we do not have with our loved ones or be grateful for the time we do have. Choose to be grateful and remember with Heaven in the equation, even death can be turned from a downer to a delight.

Colossians 3:15
"And let the peace that comes from Christ rule in your hearts. For as members of one body you are called to live in peace. And always be thankful."

Smiles Add Miles to Your Journey

Recently I went down to my woodshop and made a couple smiley face pieces for the neighbor kids. They refer to Carolyn as their honorary grandma. What is it about a child that makes us smile? Is it their lack of facades, their love of life, their innocence, or the fact they smile so brightly? Wouldn't it be great if we adults had these same traits?

I know one adult who did. So many people have spoken about Carolyn's ability to make them feel special. Carolyn listened with her whole body. When you were in her presence you knew she valued you. Her face lit up when a friend was near sending the signal that she was truly happy to see you. Her gentle spirit, empty of bias, radiated acceptance helping us feel good about ourselves no matter what was going on in our life. She was able to make people smile.

Children have many of the same qualities and they definitely can make us smile. If you are a parent you are probably thinking, "my kids don't listen like that". I have discovered they do. We just don't realize it until they have grown up. It turns out our sons, Doug (age 32) and Dan (age 27) listened a lot more than we thought, and we are extremely proud of how they processed what they heard.

Smiles add miles to the joy of our journey, so shed your facades, show a love for life, reconnect with your innocence, and smile like a child.

Luke 9:48
"Then he said to them, "Anyone who welcomes a little child like this on my behalf welcomes me, and anyone who welcomes me also welcomes my Father who sent me. Whoever is the least among you is the greatest."

Woo Hoo! What A Ride

The last two months of Carolyn's life was a flurry of living on the edge. She would not let the disease cramp her style. A plaque that hangs over the kitchen sink reads " Motto to live by— Life should not be a journey to the grave with the intention of arriving safely in an attractive and well preserved body, but rather to skid in sideways, chocolate in one hand, wine in the other, body thoroughly used up, totally worn out, and screaming, WOO HOO! What a ride."

During these months, we were on the go as much as possible, excited with what life had to offer. Many social events were planned including cabin visits. Friendships were honed to perfection. Family gathered and shared life stories filled with love and memories. Our dream vacation became reality. Literally five weeks before Carolyn passed, we signed her out of hospice and went on an Alaskan cruise. She slept a lot but enjoyed every minute. The scenery was breathtaking, the time together—priceless.

We lived like we were dying. The reality is this. All of us are dying. The only difference in our lives was that Carolyn had a pretty good idea when this would happen. What a difference this attitude made in her journey to the grave. Every moment counted, every interaction magnified. Life was fresh and precious. Fear was pushed aside to let God's love fill our hearts. Many authors have written on the concept of living life to the fullest one day at a time. I can attest to the beauty and excitement of this lifestyle. Why were we able to embrace this motto? Simply put— We believe in a God of love who has prepared a heavenly journey filled with peace. Woo Hoo, what a ride that will be!

Jude 1:21
"Await the mercy of our Lord Jesus Christ, who will bring you eternal life."

Refreshed

I love it after a storm moves through. The air is fresh, temperature down, and you can almost hear the plants say ahhh. A major storm blew into our lives when Carolyn's body crashed. She suddenly could no longer care for herself. The day before she crashed, Carolyn played the piano at the memorial service of a dear friend's husband. During the service I could see her life-blood draining and she could barely make it to the car afterwards. That was the last time she was able to leave the house. What followed was a hurricane of love. People stepped up to help, we got Carolyn set up in home hospice, and life settled into a new normal. Our two boys were here, and gobs of people stopped by to visit. We needed these things.

Our home survived the storm and is still intact; it just looks a little different. Amidst the debris cancer had created in Carolyn's body our faith stood firm and our family found peace. The air truly became fresh again. Every time someone visited Carolyn's eyes lit up as she gave a little "yeah": my social butterfly to the end. We had come to terms with the nearness of Carolyn's journey to Heaven and knew we would both be OK.

 The storm that devastated Carolyn's body was weathered and our lives changed from a stifling maze of uncertainty to a path of confidence because God promised to save us. Carolyn accepted His gift of Heaven; I accepted His gift of peace. Ahhh, I made it through the storm refreshed and ready to utilize the lessons learned from it.

Matthew 11:28-30
"Come to me, all of you who are weary and carry heavy burdens,
and I will give you rest. Take my yoke upon you. Let me teach you,
because I am humble and gentle at heart, and you will find rest for
your souls. For my yoke is easy to bear."

Restless Whispers

One of Carolyn's favorite shows was "Dancing With The Stars". Her dreams the last few nights on Earth must have been about this show. It was as if she was in a slow motion ballet of constant leg and arm motion. Rhythmically moving to an unheard melody. I wondered, "What song is she is dancing to?" Is it a gentle melody from God beckoning her closer towards Him? Or is it a song of torment with haunting strings tying her to what remains of this life? I wish I knew. She whispered the answer, but no matter how hard I listened I could not comprehend it. Carolyn's body was fading as her spirit prepared to leave.

I too was restless. A feeling of helplessness poured through my veins. I wanted to comprehend what she needed and what timetable she was on. I felt like a deaf person straining to hear a symphony. I saw the musicians on stage but could not enjoy the fruits of their labor. I cried out to God for help in coping! His answer was "trust in me, it is my music she hears." From that moment on I felt his touch on our lives. I did trust in Him. Carolyn's restless whispers were indeed a beautiful dance with Jesus in anticipation of a symphony of love awaiting her in Heaven. He will sweep her off her feet and gently set her down on the grandest of all ballroom floors, as sweet music fills the air with the glorious sounds of an angelic choir.

Psalm 143:8
"Let me hear of your unfailing love each morning,
for I am trusting you. Show me where to walk,
for I give myself to you."

Therapy Sessions

I am beginning to relate to King David as he wrote the psalms. I find myself most inspired in times of turmoil and uncertainty. It's as if God offers me a therapy session through writing. By sitting down to write I am able to evaluate and organize the jumbled thoughts of the day. As I focus on my relationship with Him the lessons learned that day are clarified. Thoughts rise above worldly hurts and grab onto the peace God offers. In these times I find Him to be a great listener. He doesn't say much, and doesn't utilize a couch, but sure gets results. I leave each session revived and reenergized, ready to find the good in each new day. Positive emotions emerge as pleasant memories flash in my brain. I have shared my love for Carolyn with the creator of life and He has responded with hope.

During the final days of Carolyn's battle with cancer, turmoil was the norm and could have spun out of control if I hadn't spent therapy time with God. These sessions resulted in writings like this that literally jumped onto the page. Writing helped clarify the lessons learned that day so I could start refreshed the next morning. In the end I came to the realization that God had chosen me to be Carolyn's earthly guide on the last leg of her journey we call life. What an honor. I did not receive any medals for my efforts. I received something even better: The knowledge that God is always available for therapy sessions.

Psalm 126:3
"Yes, the LORD has done amazing things for us!
What joy!"

Renewable Energy

One of society's biggest issues today is lowering our dependence on oil. We have discovered renewable energy options but haven't been able to make them fully cost effective. One of our biggest personal issues is lowering our energy dependence on worldly things. A renewable source has been known for over 2000 years but we don't always let it be effective. He is known as Jesus, and I am drawing a lot of power from Him lately. Carolyn and I often wondered how people without a strong faith deal with a situation like ours. Happily I do not know the answer to this question. Thank you Lord. Following is a dialog that ran through my mind about a week before she died. "Yes, Carolyn returns my smile each time she wakes. Yes, we are both totally confident that heaven waits. Yes, we would like this disease to go away, but place absolutely no blame on anyone. Yes, we have been blessed and are continually recharged by God's love for us." By drawing on His power, I was able to stay positive and trust in the final outcome.

God has placed another renewable energy source in our midst, people. To make them effective we need to open ourselves up and receive. This is a very hard thing to do, but once you realize people are God's energizers, receiving becomes a lot easier. Friends supply a necessary jolt of support, sympathy, and connection. We were not wired to go through hardships alone. By accepting the gifts of friendship we are investing into a powerful source of renewable energy.

God's love is never ending. If we tap into it we will never loose power and our light can shine forever.

Romans 8:28
"And we know that God causes everything to work together for the good of those who love God and are called according to his purpose for them."

Oh Mamma What A Day ☺

Yesterday Carolyn woke at 5 a.m., chipper and ready to go. Her boys were home and her mom was coming to spend the day. Oh what a day it was. First, a little about Florence Lorene Pickering, age 91. She napped less than Carolyn and myself, and climbs stairs like a 59 year old (that's me); During one of Carolyn's sleep times she insisted on folding and ironing three loads of laundry, and carried a glow of extreme pride throughout the day. During wake times Carolyn beamed and was more alert than she had been all week. The nausea that had been hounding her stayed away and she stayed alert much longer between naps. We listened as Florence shared stories of life during the Depression, and Carolyn growing up. Both of her grandsons had heartfelt conversations with her that brought laughter and tears. We were a family enjoying each other's company, pushing aside future worries and accepting of the gift of the present. In short, "Life was good."

At the end of the day, I found Carolyn and her mom sleeping in adjoining chairs holding hands, content and at peace with the world. The serenity of that moment will live in my memory for a lifetime. It captured the essence of Jesus holding out his arms to wrap us in His loving embrace. Why haven't we scheduled family time more often?

Jude 1:21

"Await the mercy of our Lord Jesus Christ, who will bring you eternal life. In this way, you will keep yourselves safe in God's love."

Move That Bus

I often cry when the host of Extreme Makeover Home Edition says, "move that bus". A crowd of friends cheer and for one family life is changed. We had a "move that bus" experience two weeks before Carolyn's death. On a Saturday morning, a crew of musicians/singers lifted us to a mountaintop so we could receive the grace that God was pouring out from Heaven.

Nothing in life brought Carolyn more comfort and joy than worship. On this day she was blessed, as family and friends arrived for what I told Carolyn was a party. She carefully chose a party outfit and greeted people as they arrived. Then the real party began. Unannounced, a large troupe of singers burst into the house to serenade Carolyn. People from all phases of the music program she had been active with had come to bless her. We began with this prayer: "Dear and glorious lord, we worship you and give thanks for lives filled with your love. No matter how long we live whether it is 20 years, 50 years, or 90 years, we think it is too short, yet our time on Earth is but a speck when compared to the time we will spend with you in Heaven. For this hope so lovingly offered by your son, we are truly grateful."

For the next hour we were overcome with waves of spiritual bliss that brought us closer to God. The singers bathed us in sweet melody as musicians filled the air with harmonic beauty. Tears of joy flowed down our cheeks in honor of a God that has blessed our lives beyond measure. Near the beginning Carolyn leaned over and whispered in her familiar soft voice, "I get to have my service don't I." She said this with a huge beaming smile. Carolyn had blessed so many and they in turn had blessed her. Life with true friends is priceless. Life with a God like ours is eternal. That Saturday was one of the best days of my life.

Psalm 119:114
"You are my refuge and my shield;
your word is my source of hope."

Heavenly Hospice

Our hospice experience was filled with earthly angels peacefully guiding us to a new life. I am deeply grateful for everything they did for Carolyn and myself. I am amazed at the personable efficiency each team member displayed. Every time a medication was needed, it showed up. A chair? No problem. Time for a hospital bed? Jimmy Johns couldn't have been faster. Crisis management information? Spot on. Every detail and comfort was covered however, the true value of our hospice care was found in the providers. Patience, empathy, expertise and caring surrounded them like halos. The goal of hospice care is making the transition from life to death as gentle and respectful as possible. Because these caregivers had adopted servant hearts, our team accomplished that goal.

We can learn from these people. By acting as true servants they were able to bring peace to a stressful situation— aren't we capable of doing the same? Christ was the perfect model of this behavior and look what He was able to accomplish! I believe if we adopt a hospice attitude and become true servants our lives, and the lives of those around us, can find great comfort in this world. The reality is this: We all are in a transition period from life to death. If we adopt hospice attitudes, the results will be heavenly.

Colossians 3:12
"Since God chose you to be the holy people he loves, you must clothe yourselves with tenderhearted mercy, kindness, humility, gentleness, and patience."

Free Trial

Many products are promoted by offering a free trial. God provided us with His version of a free trial. By keeping Carolyn healthy, despite the chemotherapy, for over four years we were granted the opportunity to "live like we are dying". It worked wonders on our relationship and outlook on life. I love this mindset so much I have ordered a lifetime subscription for myself.

I also received a second free trial offer. The offer of experiencing what life would be like once Carolyn was in Heaven and I was still on Earth. One of the highlights of each summer was an all day outing we call the Varner Classic. Friends of 50 plus years gather in Big Lake Minnesota to golf, eat, and fellowship. When the day of the Varner classic arrived. I went— alone. A dear friend stayed with Carolyn while I went out and played. God offered me a trial run of my future and it worked like a charm. As I passed familiar spots on the drive I remembered times past. The café in Monticello, the turn we missed one year, and the spot a tornado ripped across the freeway. Valued memories of times past. We all missed Carolyn's presence during the day but life and fellowship went on. I was comfortable and accepted by my friends as a single. It comforted me to know I would be able to carry on my social life. The best part of the day, however, was the drive home, because this was a trial and I was able to travel back into the open arms of my love. Carolyn's cancer prayer was 1 Thessalonians 5:16-18, *"Always be joyful. Never stop praying. Be thankful in all circumstances, for this is God's will for you who belong to Christ Jesus."* Boy did this ring true for me.

Proverbs 24:14
"In the same way, wisdom is sweet to your soul.
If you find it, you will have a bright future,
and your hopes will not be cut short."

Inspiration

These devotions have been popping into my head for over fifteen years. I considered publication many times but it just never seemed finished. Now I know why. The nucleus for the final chapter is being written, as Carolyn is getting ready to move on to Heaven. The inspiration I often receive from God is flowing like our Minnesota Rivers this year, high and fast.

We are now in the care stage— the beginning of the final lap. Today we turned our beautiful living room, with views of waterfalls and rock gardens through large picture windows, into my queen's throne room. A hospital bed arrived, and God showed his presence. To set Carolyn up in the living room it required a commode because the bathrooms are on different levels. Our neighbor Michelle called to see how things were going and I mentioned I was searching for a room divider. She sent e-mails out to friends and one hour later a beautiful bamboo divider was in place. She has it all now: A live in butler, a room that is all rooms in one, friends who continue to bless us, and a God who is getting ready to welcome her home. In some ways life doesn't get better than this. Say goodbye to a dark bedroom and say hello to a luxury suite that fits Carolyn's personality. "Bright and cheery." Once settled, Carolyn remarked, "You know if it wasn't for the circumstances, this would be fun."

I often find God inspires me most when life is tweaked out of the norm. As I spend time with Carolyn these final days life is anything but normal. Yet we both feel closer to God now than any other time in our lives. He is the master of inspiration, He knows exactly when we need it. It is our job to recognize His voice and turn His inspiration into action.

Job 37:5
"God's voice is glorious in the thunder.
We can't even imagine the greatness of his power."

Sweet Music

About midway through the home hospice experience, Carolyn had a rare breakdown; huge tears flowed down her cheeks. When I asked why she said, "My piano, what is going to happen to it?" She knew the boys and myself do not play. We thought long and hard but couldn't come up with a solution. The next day a dear friend and her daughter visited bearing a beautiful bouquet of flowers. As we discussed her daughter's coming fall she mentioned piano lessons. I asked if she had a piano and she said "no". Our hearts jumped for joy and Carolyn started bawling. Her precious piano had found a home. This piano has glorious history. Carolyn lost her dad when she was eight and her mom used some Social Security money from his death to purchase it. All three Pickering kids learned how to play piano on it. We were given the piano in the late 70's and it has provided comfort since then. Carolyn is most at peace when playing. She put in thousands of hours, practicing and selecting worship songs. It hosted many sessions of choir and small group rehearsals. It was her "go to" place when stressed. In short Carolyn and her piano were close friends.

This is such a God story. When we are at our lowest He is often at His highest. Providing us with hope to counteract despair is something He is really good at. That night we cried again as we thanked God for providing hope. His constant care is sweet music to our hearts.

Galatians 3:5
"I ask you again, does God give you the Holy Spirit and work miracles among you because you obey the law? Of course not! It is because you believe the message you heard about Christ."

"The Cat's in the Cradle"

Do you know this 1974 Harry Chapin song? Every time I hear it I think of my boys. I am hearing it in my head right now and crying tears of joy. My boys are just like me. Dan and I had a great faith talk yesterday that brought me comfort. He gets it. God is good and mom is going to be okay. Then I read Doug's post on <u>Caring Bridge</u>. "I just wanted to thank all the friends and family who have been so comforting and caring to us. Although mom's physical presence on Earth may be limited I am confident mom's legacy will live on forever. Our family has always been very close and in times like this there is nothing that can replace the love and comfort of our family and friends along with strong faith in God. Although Sarah and I are miles away from home, we feel comforted by the fact that mom is always surrounded by people that love her and the Lord is waiting on her arrival. My father has been patient, loving, kind and a great leader all these years. These past few weeks have really shown me what mom got to see all these years. In the past few weeks everything has fallen into place. Since treatment ended earlier this year mom told us and prepared us that she will probably not see her next birthday in October. These words were devastating. As we look back we now realize it was a true blessing. We have cherished every phone call; e-mail, Skype, day and weekend that we had got to spend together. We love you with all our heart. Mom, words alone cannot express how much I love you. You are my angel, my hero and dearest friend. I feel you close to me and will always be able to close my eyes and feel your arms around me, with a big smile, strong hug and encouraging words. I love you so much. Thank you for always being there for me. You have made me who I am today."

There are tears on the keyboard as I type. What a gift they are to us. A parent's goal in life is to instill just enough wisdom in their children to help them be successful and happy. Both Dan and Doug have exceeded our hopes and have made us proud.

Galatians 4:6
"Because we are his children, God has sent the Spirit of his Son into our hearts, prompting us to call out, "Abba, Father."

Coming Home

At noon on August 26, 2011, Carolyn's breathing changed and I knew it was time to call my oldest son Douglas, home. Douglas lives just south of Milwaukee. He was able to get a flight that arrived at 9:30 p.m. Dan and I sat with Carolyn all day but she never woke up. The longest hour of my life was from 9 to 10 p.m. that night. Dan had gone to pick up Doug at the airport. I held her hand and fervently prayed that she would hold on until they returned. Eighteen years before this, I had missed my mom's passing by minutes. I didn't want them to do the same.

My prayers were answered. Doug and Dan arrived and the three of us had a couple hours together with mom. Carolyn's family had made it home in time to help usher her into her new home— what a gift. At 1 a.m. she peacefully breathed her last breath in this world and opened her spiritual eyes to see Jesus face to face. Even in death Carolyn showed no fear. At 2 a.m. our longtime friends and small group partners joined hands with us around her bed and prayed prayers of praise and thanksgiving to the God of mercy and love. At 4 a.m. the people from the cremation society arrived to take her body away. It was done.

At 6 a.m. God sealed the deal for me by providing a glorious sunrise. (The cover picture for this book was taken from my front door step on that morning) He was telling me "all is well." Even in my darkest hour, the beauty of God's light filled me with hope. A huge piece of my life was gone yet I knew God would help me fill that gaping hole with peace.

2 Samuel 22:29
"O LORD, you are my lamp.
The LORD lights up my darkness."

Fear Not!

Christ's last words on this Earth are recorded in John 19:30, *"It is finished!"* At first the disciples thought this meant Jesus was gone and no longer available to them. We are blessed to know the rest of the story. Jesus lives on, and because of Him so do we.

On August 27, 2011, Carolyn checked into a new suite, one chosen just for her in the presence of God. Carolyn's mantra has always been ***fear not***. From this day forward she doesn't have to work to make this come true. She is totally fear free and able to lift her voice in praise. Her journey has moved to the high road. We are still on the low road but have been given a lot of survival skills to help us find her in Heaven. We have a God who loves us and promised to help us in times of need. Cry a little; mourn a little; spill a little grief; but no matter what, *"Fear Not"* for God is with you always. God has granted me a peace that passes my understanding. I will not fear for He is with me and Carolyn lives on in my heart. I pray that you will also experience the joy of knowing we have a God that will never give us more than we can handle.

I have a shirt that says, "There is no finish line". Now I know what that means. Carolyn isn't finished because she lives on in Heaven. I am not finished because I must rebuild my life without her physical presence. We, as a couple, are not finished because I can reach into my memory and fill my heart with her love. Christ came to Earth to save us. Because of Him life has no finish line. So fear not and move forward in peace.

2 Timothy 4:7-8
"I have fought the good fight, I have finished the race, and I have remained faithful. And now the prize awaits me—the crown of righteousness, which the Lord, the righteous Judge, will give me on the day of his return."

Between Two Worlds

I wrote the following journal a few days before Carolyn passed away. "I am convinced the dying process is hardest on those who are left behind. Carolyn is no longer the quick-witted person I adore. Don't get me wrong my love is just as strong, maybe even stronger than before, but I'm greedy and want her whole. I find myself fighting back frustration as communication becomes more difficult. She wants a shower but it is not physically possible. She processes slowly and I have to repeat myself. Her voice is a whisper and I struggle to hear. Lord, give me the patience that my Carolyn deserves. Through all of this she has a peaceful glow about her. She sleeps with a smile and is content. In her eyes, life is good. I believe she is prepping herself for Heaven (Boy does she know how to prepare for a party)."

While not all journeys to Heaven are as smooth and pain free as Carolyn's, I think God grants peace to all who ask for it. Her doctor once told me there is only so much medicine can do. The human spirit can accomplish things beyond our understanding. The view from my world was one of uncertainty and loss. The view from her world was heavenly. The peace she experienced throughout the cancer journey was granted to her because she asked for it. I also have sought God's peace. Since her death He has showered me with it. All I had to do was ask. This peace acts like a bridge between two worlds linking comfort in this one with eternal joy in the next.

John 14: 27
"I am leaving you with a gift—peace of mind and heart.
And the peace I give is a gift the world cannot give.
So don't be troubled or afraid."

Grief Leads to Hope

A wild animal known for its mournful cry, the timber wolf can be dangerous, but it also can bring a sense of awe and appreciation to life. Like grief, the timber wolf is a natural part of God's creation. It is a survivor, and if cornered, will lash out. Grief will do the same. Blaming God for your troubles is one way we attempt to corner grief. "Why me Lord?" "My wife was such a good person! I don't understand why you allowed this to happen!" By going down this road you close communication with God from your end and block His help. You become me-centered and grief's pack mates, anger, sorrow, and depression join up in an attempt to consume your life.

If you feed a timber wolf you're asking for trouble. It will learn there is an easy meal available and continue to come back day after day. In the same way, by feeding grief you endanger yourself. Dwelling on the "what-ifs," "how will I's," and "how can I's," feed grief and invite it back day after day.

But consider this; can grief actually make your life richer? The timber wolf in its natural state is a majestic animal with a lifestyle focused on survival. The wolf relies on its God-given tools to survive. Shouldn't we do the same? God has given us the tools to handle the loss of a loved one. The most precious of these is faith that your loved one is now cradled in His arms, resting in a place infinitely better than the one left behind.

Finally, like us, timber wolves interact as a community. If hurt or injured the pack will care for the wolf in need. Communal grief brings people together, heightens their awareness of each other, and strengthens bonds. This is a part of the grieving process and a necessary reminder that we can't do it alone. If we approach grief with respect as an integral part of God's world and understand both its dangers and strengths, it can help us recover to reclaim our hope.

John 16:22
" So you have sorrow now, but I will see you again; then you will rejoice, and no one can rob you of that joy."

Better Than Duct Tape

I love duct tape and I'm not alone. Books have been written about it and stories of innovative uses abound. Many people have avoided disaster by having a roll of duct tape handy. What makes it so valuable? It is flexible, allowing us to form it to almost any object. It sticks well, and holds up in a large range of environmental conditions. Its fiber mesh makes it strong yet easy to use. Few products in our world have been used in more diverse situations than duct tape.

The love of Jesus is like that duct tape. Books have been written about it. Stories of life change due to its power abound, and many people have been spared disaster by its comfort. His love is flexible enough to be custom fit to any person's needs. Anyone desiring his love receives it in a personally tailored way. The results of accepting God's love stick in our hearts and hold through all kinds of situations. God's love is stronger than anything the world can throw at it. A weaving of the Holy Spirit into its fibers strengthens this love while making it readily available anytime anywhere. No product made by man has been used in more diverse situations with better results than the love of Jesus Christ.

Since Carolyn's death I have used God's duct tape almost daily. It is a constant I can trust in. All I have to do is ask for help and He unrolls just the right amount to fix the situation. God's love is better than duct tape.

Matthew 21:22
"You can pray for anything, and if you have faith,
you will receive it."

190

Life is Grand

On one of my first vacations as a widower I visited friends in Phoenix Arizona. A part of that trip included four days of exploring northern Arizona by myself. There I experienced beautiful rock formations, desert landscaping, and the Grand Canyon. The rock formations around Sedona are a result of many years of deposition creating great layers of rock filled with beautiful colors. The desert, seemingly barren, was anything but that when experienced at a personal level. The Grand Canyon, a tear resulting from massive erosion, has its history exposed for everyone to witness.

It hit me that all three of these natural wonders related to my life. The colorful rock formations around Sedona are like the many experiences with Carolyn cemented together painting the landscape of our lives. With her gone, my life seems like the desert surrounding the Sedona highlands. Barren and drab filled with harsh realities. Yet if you look closely, there is great beauty in the desert and the organisms that live there are survivors. That beauty exists in my life also. Thorns may be more common now, but I have learned to survive.

As I sat gazing over the Grand Canyon with awe and wonderment I realized it's beauty is a result of a loss. Thousands of feet of the Arizona Plateau have been ripped away and moved to new location never to return, leaving a gaping canyon that we call grand. Thousands of years of history are exposed waiting for us to gaze upon. This part of Arizona has new beauty as a result of that loss. Like Northern Arizona, I too have been reworked to create a new landscape. There is a canyon in my soul with our shared history exposed for viewing as a reminder of the beauty still in my life. God sure knew what he was doing when he set the forces of nature to work in creating northern Arizona. God also knew what he was doing when he created us. From birth, to death, to everlasting life, life itself is simply grand.

John 17:24

"Father, I want these whom you have given me to be with me where I am. Then they can see all the glory you gave me because you loved me even before the world began!"

A New Coat of Paint

Recently I spent a week at a canoe base camp on Lake of the Woods, to help paint a cabin in dire need of a new coat of paint. As we power-washed, the old paint disintegrated and spider webs flew. Under the mass of webs and old paint the original cedar became exposed. Most of it was in good condition but in some spots rot had turned it into a mushy sponge-like mass. Then we started painting. With each stroke of the brush the cabin was transformed from ratty to refreshed. The very next day we arrived to find hundreds of cobwebs. The spiders that live on this cabin had a busy night.

Recovering from loss is like this cabin. Every now and then we need to strip the old ways off and refresh our souls. As we power-wash the soot of sorrow out of our system, our true inner self is exposed in the form God intended. At the same time we need to toss the cobwebs of grief out the window so we can focus on Him. Then comes the paint. With each stroke of prayer we reconnect with our savior. With each act of service we spread some humility. With each round of worship we roll on a protective coat against grief. We are refreshed and joy is restored.

Beware however, the cobwebs of life will return. After all we live in a hectic world. Hopefully the new coat of paint will help you navigate this world in a way that reflects Christ love for you. Continue to pray, maintain your humility, and worship often. These will prevent the cobwebs from forming too fast.

When your life is in need of a new coat of paint, give it one while you are still solid. Once the rot of depression sets in, it is difficult to dig out, and that requires more than a new coat of paint to restore.

2 Corinthians 5:17
"This means that anyone who belongs to Christ has become a new person. The old life is gone; a new life has begun!"

Sweet and Sour Chicken

One of my favorite Chinese dishes is sweet and sour chicken. I have always had a sweet tooth and it gets satisfied. A hint of sour tempers the sweetness allowing me to eat more :). Carolyn's journey is similar. So many positive things occurred in the five years leading up to her death an entire book couldn't hold them. The sweet taste of love satisfied my craving for her each and every day as we lived these days knowing each one was a gift from God. Now a dash of sour has been added. To watch her melt away was painful and even though I prepared for life without her it has left a sour taste in my heart. Like a good Chinese restaurant God has made sure the sweet memories of our life together overpower the sourness of her loss. I can draw on His love and the many memories with my sweet Carolyn to get me through when times seem bad. These memories are like the oven that cooks a savory meal. As the memories flit through my mind or across my computer screen, they combine the flavors of our life experiences. These in turn blend with my present life to feed my desire for her. When fully cooked, this memory meal restores balance and gives me a satisfied feeling. Thank you Lord for the food you sent in the form of your love. It's the best sweet and sour chicken I have ever tasted.

John 6:27
"But don't be so concerned about perishable things like food. Spend your energy seeking the eternal life that the Son of Man can give you. For God the Father has given me the seal of his approval."

The Antidote

An antidote is a substance that can counteract a poison. Fear and worry can be like a poison in our lives. Both paralyze hope and invite anxiety. The "what if's" and "why me's" combine to block out happiness as they drain our joy.

Thankfully we have an antidote for this. It's called trust. God is trustworthy and can be counted on to help us through tough times. Ask him for help and he will deliver. My wife Carolyn learned this lesson while lying on a gurney preparing to have an MRI to search for the cancer. Her mind was a jumbled mess of unknowns. Then it hit her. "I could pray." She did, and the fear melted away. She trusted that her faith would be enough to cut through the negativity, and it did. The prognosis was bad (cancer on her spine and near her pelvis) but the results were simply amazing. She was pain free through four years of chemotherapy, maintained a positive attitude, and never let fear creep into her life. Joy, hope, and peace surrounded her throughout the cancer journey. It is also working for me. Will it work for you? Trust in God that it will.

Sometimes God works like an anti-venom, which is a product that produces antibodies to combat a poison. He places people and situations in your life that counteract the poison of earthly events. Maybe it will be someone who has experienced your situation and conquered it. Maybe it's a professional trained to deal with what ails you. Maybe it's just a good friend, or family member. By reaching out to people you build "antibodies" to combat whatever is poisoning your life. God has a huge arsenal of powerful antidotes, which He offers freely. All you have to do is pray, then trust in His love.

"No more fear— No more worry"
It sounds like Heaven on Earth.

Isaiah 41:10
"Don't be afraid, for I am with you. Don't be discouraged, for I am your God. I will strengthen you and help you."

All Good Things Must Come to an End

If anyone ever gives you this line, reject it in memory of Carolyn Kranz. She was good to the deepest part of her soul, and she didn't come to an end, only a new beginning. This devotional book, however, must come to an end. I thank you from the bottom of my heart for entering my world by reading this book. If you liked it please pass it on.

A wonderful team helped Carolyn transition to Heaven in royal fashion. Family and friends surrounded us with love, as the hospice team orchestrated a peaceful passing. I truly felt the presence of God throughout the journey. I can feel Carolyn looking down from Heaven whispering the same thing God spoke at the beginning of creation. "It is good." I have never felt so loved or so loving.

I have had the privilege of experiencing God's presence in my life. I pray that you too have discovered the beauty of walking with God as you mosey along your life trails.

Since her death, I miss my sweet Carolyn. While touches of grief have ached in my heart, I have never felt alone. God has been by my side, plus I have been able to close my eyes to visualize the love of my life smiling. Both of their presences have soothed the pain and restored my resolve to continue saying, **"Life is Good."**

Thank you God for being so loving
as you provide the abundance of peace I feel.
Dave Kranz.

Psalm 136: 26
"Give thanks to the God of heaven.
His faithful love endures forever."

www.ingramcontent.com/pod-product-compliance
Lightning Source LLC
LaVergne TN
LVHW051233080426
835513LV00016B/1565